THE ESSAYS OF ARTHUR SCHOPENHAUER: ON HUMAN NATURE.

ARTHUR SCHOPENHAUER

Paperback: 978-936205648-1
Hardback: 978-936205452-4
eBook:978-936205898-0

Any references to historical events, real people, or real places are used fictitiously. Names, characters, and places are products of the author's imagination.

Printed by:

Sanage Publishing House LLP
Mumbai, India

sanagepublishing@gmail.com

Arthur Schopenhauer (22 February 1788 – 21 September 1860) was a German philosopher. He is best known for his 1818 work "The World as Will and Representation (expanded in 1844)", which characterizes the phenomenal world as the product of a blind noumenal will.

He was among the first thinkers in Western philosophy to share and affirm significant tenets of Indian philosophy, such as asceticism, denial of the self, and the notion of the world-as-appearance. His work has been described as an exemplary manifestation of philosophical pessimism.

CONTENTS

TRANSLATOR'S PREFACE.

The following essays are drawn from the chapters entitled *Zur Ethik and Zur Rechtslehre und Politik* which are to be found both in Schopenhauer's Parerga and in his posthumous writings. As in my previous volumes, so also in this, I have omitted a few passages which appeared to me to be either antiquated or no longer of any general interest. For convenience' sake I have divided the original chapters into sections, which I have had to name; and I have also had to invent a title which should express their real scope. The reader will find that it is not so much Ethics and Politics that are here treated, as human nature itself in various aspects.

T. Bailey Saunders.

HUMAN NATURE.

Truths of the physical order may possess much external significance, but internal significance they have none. The latter is the privilege of intellectual and moral truths, which are concerned with the objectivation of the will in its highest stages, whereas physical truths are concerned with it in its lowest.

For example, if we could establish the truth of what up till now is only a conjecture, namely, that it is the action of the sun which produces thermoelectricity at the equator; that this produces terrestrial magnetism; and that this magnetism, again, is the cause of the aurora borealis, these would be truths externally of great, but internally of little, significance. On the other hand, examples of internal significance are furnished by all great and true philosophical systems; by the catastrophe of every good tragedy; nay, even by the observation of human conduct in the extreme manifestations of its morality and immorality, of its good and its evil character. For all these are expressions of that reality which takes outward shape as the world, and which, in the highest stages of its objectivation, proclaims its innermost nature.

To say that the world has only a physical and not a moral significance is the greatest and most pernicious of all errors, the fundamental blunder, the real perversity of mind and temper; and, at bottom, it is doubtless the tendency which faith personifies as Anti-Christ. Nevertheless, in spite of all religions—and they are systems which one and all maintain the opposite and seek to establish it in their mythical way—this fundamental error never becomes quite extinct, but raises its head from time to time afresh, until universal indignation compels it to hide itself once more.

Yet, however certain we may feel of the moral significance of life and the world, to explain and illustrate it, and to resolve the contradiction between this significance and the world as it is, form a task of great difficulty; so great, indeed, as to make it possible that it has remained for me to exhibit the true and only genuine and sound basis of morality everywhere and at all times effective, together with the results to which it leads. The actual facts of morality are too much on my side for me to fear that my theory can ever be replaced or upset by any other.

However, so long as even my ethical system continues to be ignored by the professorial world, it is Kant's moral principle that prevails in the universities. Among its various forms the one which is most in favour at present is "the dignity of man." I have already exposed the absurdity of this doctrine in my treatise on the Foundation of Morality.{1} Therefore I will only say here that if the question were asked on what the alleged dignity of man rests, it would not be long before the answer was made that it rests upon his morality. In other words, his morality rests upon his dignity, and his dignity rests upon his morality.

{Footnote 1: § 8.}

But apart from this circular argument it seems to me that the idea of dignity can be applied only in an ironical sense to a being whose will is so sinful, whose intellect is so limited, whose body is so weak and perishable as man's. How shall a man be proud, when his conception is a crime, his birth a penalty, his life a labour and death a necessity!—

Quid superbit homo? cujus conceptio culpa,

Nasci poena, labor vita, necesse mori!

Therefore, in opposition to the above-mentioned form of the Kantian principle, I should be inclined to lay down the following rule: When you come into contact with a man, no matter whom, do not attempt an objective appreciation of him according to his worth and dignity. Do not consider his bad will, or his narrow understanding and perverse ideas; as the former may easily lead you to hate and the latter to despise him; but fix your attention only upon his sufferings, his needs, his anxieties, his pains. Then you will always feel your kinship with him; you will sympathize with him and instead of hatred or contempt you will experience the commiseration that alone is the peace to which the Gospel calls us. The way to keep down hatred and contempt is certainly not to look for a man's alleged "dignity," but, on the contrary, to regard him as an object of pity.

The Buddhists, as the result of the more profound views which they entertain on ethical and metaphysical subjects, start from the cardinal vices and not the cardinal virtues, since the virtues make their appearance only as the contraries or negations of the vices. According to Schmidt's History of the Eastern Mongolians the cardinal vices in the Buddhist scheme are four: Lust, Indolence, Anger, and Avarice. But probably instead of Indolence, we should read Pride; for so it stands in the Lettres édifiantes et curieuses,{1} where Envy, or Hatred, is added as a fifth. I am confirmed in correcting the statement of the excellent Schmidt by the fact that my rendering agrees with the doctrine of the Sufis, who are certainly under the influence of the Brahmins and Buddhists. The Sufis also maintain that there are four cardinal vices, and they arrange them in very striking pairs, so that Lust appears in connection with Avarice, and Anger with Pride. The four cardinal virtues opposed to them would be Chastity and Generosity, together with Gentleness and Humility.

{Footnote 1: Edit, of 1819, vol. vi., p. 372.}

When we compare these profound ideas of morality, as they are entertained by oriental nations, with the celebrated cardinal virtues of Plato, which have been recapitulated again and again—Justice, Valour, Temperance, and Wisdom—it is plain that the latter are not based on any clear, leading idea, but are chosen on grounds that are superficial and, in part, obviously false. Virtues must be qualities of the will, but Wisdom is chiefly an attribute of the Intellect. {Greek: Sophrosynae}, which Cicero translates Temperantia, is a very indefinite and ambiguous word, and it admits, therefore, of a variety of applications: it may mean discretion, or abstinence, or keeping a level head. Courage is not a virtue at all; although sometimes it is a servant or instrument of virtue; but it is just as ready to become the servant of the greatest villainy. It is really a quality of temperament. Even Geulinx (in the preface to this Ethics) condemned the Platonic virtues and put the following in their place: Diligence, Obedience, Justice, and Humility, which are obviously bad. The Chinese distinguish five cardinal virtues: Sympathy, Justice, Propriety, Wisdom, and Sincerity. The virtues of Christianity are theological, not cardinal: Faith, Love, and Hope.

Fundamental disposition towards others, assuming the character either of Envy or of Sympathy, is the point at which the moral virtues and vices of mankind first diverge. These two diametrically opposite qualities exist in every man; for they spring from the inevitable comparison which he draws between his own lot and that of others. According as the result of this comparison affects his individual character does the one or the other of these qualities become the source and principle of all his action. Envy builds the wall between Thee and Me thicker and stronger; Sympathy makes it slight and transparent; nay, sometimes it pulls down the wall altogether and then the distinction between self and not-self vanishes.

Valour, which has been mentioned as a virtue, or rather the

Courage on which it is based (for valour is only courage in war), deserves a closer examination. The ancients reckoned Courage among the virtues, and cowardice among the vices; but there is no corresponding idea in the Christian scheme, which makes for charity and patience, and in its teaching forbids all enmity or even resistance. The result is that with the moderns Courage is no longer a virtue. Nevertheless, it must be admitted that cowardice does not seem to be very compatible with any nobility of character—if only for the reason that it betrays an over-great apprehension about one's own person.

Courage, however, may also be explained as a readiness to meet ills that threaten at the moment, in order to avoid greater ills that lie in the future, whereas cowardice does the contrary. But this readiness is of the same quality as patience, for patience consists in the clear consciousness that greater evils than those which are present, and that any violent attempt to flee from or guard against the ills we have may bring the others upon us. Courage, then, would be a kind of patience; and since it is patience that enables us to practice forbearance and self-control, Courage is, through the medium of patience, at least akin to virtue.

But perhaps Courage admits of being considered from a higher point of view. The fear of death may in every case be traced to a deficiency in that natural philosophy—natural, and therefore resting on mere feeling—which gives a man the assurance that he exists in everything outside him just as much as in his own person; so that the death of his person can do him little harm. But it is just this very assurance that would give a man heroic Courage; and therefore, as the reader will recollect from my Ethics, Courage comes from the same source as the virtues of Justice and Humanity. This is, I admit, to take a very high view of the matter; but apart from it I cannot well explain why cowardice seems contemptible, and personal courage a noble and sublime thing; for no lower point of view enables me to see why a finite individual who is everything to himself—nay, who is himself even the very fundamental condition of the existence of the rest of the world—should not put his own preservation above every other aim. It is, then, an insufficient explanation of Courage to make it rest only on utility, to give it an empirical and not a transcendental character. It may have been for some such reason that Calderon once uttered a skeptical but remarkable opinion in regard to Courage, nay, actually denied its reality; and put his denial into the mouth of a wise old minister, addressing his young sovereign. "Although," he observed, "natural fear is operative in all alike, a man may be brave in not letting it be seen; and it is this that constitutes Courage":

> *Que aunque el natural temor*
> *En todos obra igualmente,*
> *No mostrarle es ser valiente*
> *Y esto es lo que hace el valor.{1}*

{Footnote 1: La Hija del Aire, ii., 2.}

In regard to the difference which I have mentioned between the ancients and the moderns in their estimate of Courage as a virtue, it must be remembered that by Virtue, virtus, {Greek: aretae}, the ancients understood every excellence or quality that was praiseworthy in itself, it might be moral or intellectual, or possibly only physical. But when Christianity demonstrated that the fundamental tendency of life was moral, it was moral superiority alone than henceforth attached to the notion of Virtue. Meanwhile the earlier usage still survived in the elder Latinists, and also in Italian writers, as is proved by the well-known meaning of the word virtuoso. The special attention of students should be drawn to this wider range of the idea of Virtue amongst the ancients, as otherwise it might easily be a source of secret perplexity. I may recommend two passages preserved for us by Stobaeus, which will serve this purpose. One of them is apparently from the Pythagorean philosopher Metopos, in which the fitness of every bodily member is declared to be a virtue. The other pronounces that the virtue of a shoemaker is to make good shoes. This may also serve to explain why it is that in the ancient scheme of ethics virtues and vices are mentioned which find no place in ours.

As the place of Courage amongst the virtues is a matter of doubt, so is that of Avarice amongst the vices. It must not, however, be confounded with greed, which is the most immediate meaning of the Latin word avaritia. Let us then draw up and examine the arguments pro et contra in regard to Avarice and leave the final judgment to be formed by every man for himself.

On the one hand it is argued that it is not Avarice, which is a vice, but extravagance, its opposite. Extravagance springs from a brutish limitation to the present moment, in comparison with which the future, existing as it does only in thought, is as nothing. It rests upon the illusion that sensual pleasures possess a positive or real value. Accordingly, future need and misery is the price at which the spendthrift purchases pleasures that are empty, fleeting, and often no more than imaginary; or else feeds his vain, stupid self-conceit on the bows and scrapes of parasites who laugh at him in secret, or on the gaze of the mob and those who envy his magnificence. We should, therefore, shun the spendthrift as though he had the plague, and on discovering his vice break with him betimes, in order that later on, when the consequences of his extravagance ensue, we may neither have to help to bear them, nor, on the other hand, have to play the part of the friends of Timon of Athens.

At the same time, it is not to be expected that he who foolishly squanders his own fortune will leave another man's intact, if it should chance to be committed to his keeping; nay, sui profusus and alieni appetens are by Sallust very rightly conjoined. Hence it is that extravagance leads not only to impoverishment but also to crime; and crime amongst the moneyed classes is almost always the result of extravagance. It is accordingly with justice that the

Koran declares all spendthrifts to be "brothers of Satan."

But it is superfluity that Avarice brings in its train, and when was superfluity ever unwelcome? That must be a good vice which has good consequences. Avarice proceeds upon the principle that all pleasure is only negative in its operation and that the happiness which consists of a series of pleasures is a chimaera; that, on the contrary, it is pains which are positive and extremely real. Accordingly, the avaricious man foregoes the former in order that he may be the better preserved from the latter, and thus it is that bear and forbear—sustine et abstine—is his maxim. And because he knows, further, how inexhaustible are the possibilities of misfortune, and how innumerable the paths of danger, he increases the means of avoiding them, in order, if possible, to surround himself with a triple wall of protection. Who, then, can say where precaution against disaster begins to be exaggerated? He alone who knows where the malignity of fate reaches its limit. And even if precaution were exaggerated it is an error which at the most would hurt the man who took it, and not others. If he will never need the treasures which he lays up for himself, they will one day benefit others whom nature has made less careful. That until then he withdraws the money from circulation is no misfortune; for money is not an article of consumption: it only represents the good things which a man may actually possess and is not one itself. Coins are only counters; their value is what they represent; and what they represent cannot be withdrawn from circulation. Moreover, by holding back the money, the value of the remainder which is in circulation is enhanced by precisely the same amount. Even though it be the case, as is said, that many a miser comes in the end to love money itself for its own sake, it is equally certain that many a spendthrift, on the other hand, loves spending and squandering for no better reason. Friendship with a miser is not only without danger, but it is profitable, because of the great advantages it can bring. For it is doubtless those who are nearest and dearest to the miser who on his death will reap the fruits of the self-control which he exercised; but even in his lifetime, too, something may be expected of him in cases of great need. At any rate one can always hope for more from him than from the spendthrift, who has lost his all and is himself helpless and in debt. Mas da el duro que el desnudo, says a Spanish proverb; the man who has a hard heart will give more than the man who has an empty purse. The upshot of all this is that Avarice is not a vice.

On the other side, it may be said that Avarice is the quintessence of all vices. When physical pleasures seduce a man from the right path, it is his sensual nature—the animal part of him—which is at fault. He is carried away by its attractions, and, overcome by the impression of the moment, he acts without thinking of the consequences. When, on the other hand, he is brought by age or bodily weakness to the condition in which the vices that he could never abandon end by abandoning him and his capacity for physical pleasure dies—if he turns to Avarice, the intellectual desire survives the sensual. Money, which represents all the good things of this world, and is these good things in the abstract, now becomes the dry trunk overgrown with all the dead lusts of the flesh, which are egoism in the abstract. They come to life again in the love of the Mammon. The transient pleasure of the senses has become a deliberate and calculated lust of money, which, like that to which it is directed, is symbolical in its nature, and, like it, indestructible.

This obstinate love of the pleasures of the world—a love which, as it were, outlives itself; this utterly incorrigible sin, this refined and sublimated desire of the flesh, is the abstract form in which all lusts are concentrated, and to which it stands like a general idea to individual particulars. Accordingly, Avarice is the voice of age, just as extravagance is the voice of youth.

This disputatio in utramque partem—this debate for and against—is certainly calculated to drive us into accepting the juste milieu morality of Aristotle; a conclusion that is also supported by the following consideration.

Every human perfection is allied to a defect into which it threatens to pass; but it is also true that every defect is allied to a perfection. Hence it is that if, as often happens, we make a mistake about a man, it is because at the beginning of our acquaintance with him we confound his defects with the kinds of perfection to which they are allied. The cautious man seems to us a coward; the economical man, a miser; the spendthrift seems liberal; the rude fellow, downright and sincere; the foolhardy person looks as if he were going to work with a noble self-confidence; and so on in many other cases.

No one can live among men without feeling drawn again and again to the tempting supposition that moral baseness and intellectual incapacity are closely connected, as though they both sprang direct from one source. That that, however, is not so, I have shown in detail.{1} That it seems to be so is merely due to the fact that both are so often found together; and the circumstance is to be explained by the very frequent occurrence of each of them, so that it may easily happen for both to be compelled to live under one roof. At the same time, it is not to be denied that they play into each other's hands to their mutual benefit; and it is this that produces the very unedifying spectacle which only too many men exhibit, and that makes the world to go as it goes. A man who is unintelligent is very likely to show his perfidy, villainy, and malice, whereas a clever man understands how to conceal these qualities. And how often, on the other hand, does a perversity of heart prevent a man from seeing truths which his intelligence is quite capable of grasping!

{Footnote 1: In my chief work, vol. ii., ch. xix,}

Nevertheless, let no one boast. Just as every man, though he be the greatest genius, has very definite limitations in some one sphere of knowledge and thus attests his common origin with the essentially perverse and stupid mass of mankind, so also has every man something in his nature which is positively evil. Even the best, nay the noblest, character will sometimes surprise us by isolated traits of depravity; as though it were to acknowledge his kinship with the human race, in which villainy—nay, cruelty—is to be found in that degree. For it was just in virtue of this evil in him, this bad principle, that of necessity he became a man. And for the same reason the world in general is what my clear mirror of it has shown it to be.

But in spite of all this the difference even between one man and another is incalculably great, and many a one would be horrified to see another as he really is. Oh, for some Asmodeus of morality, to make not only roofs and walls transparent to his favourites but also to lift the veil of dissimulation, fraud, hypocrisy, pretence, falsehood and deception, which is spread over all things! to show how little true honesty there is in the world, and how often, even where it is least to be expected, behind all the exterior outwork of virtue, secretly and in the innermost recesses, unrighteousness sits at the helm! It is just on this account that so many men of the better kind have four-footed friends: for, to be sure, how is a man to get relief from the endless dissimulation, falsity, and malice of mankind, if there were no dogs into whose honest faces he can look without distrust?

For what is our civilised world but a big masquerade? where you meet knights, priests, soldiers, men of learning, barristers, clergymen, philosophers, and I don't know what all! But they are not what they pretend to be; they are only masks, and, as a rule, behind the masks you will find moneymakers. One man, I suppose, puts on the mask of law, which he has borrowed for the purpose from a barrister, only in order to be able to give another man a sound drubbing; a second has chosen the mask of patriotism and the public welfare with a similar intent; a third takes religion or purity of doctrine. For all sorts of purposes men have often put on the mask of philosophy, and even of philanthropy, and I know not what besides. Women have a smaller choice. As a rule, they avail themselves of the mask of morality, modesty, domesticity, and humility. Then there are general masks, without any particular character attaching to them like dominoes. They may be met with everywhere; and of this sort is the strict rectitude, the courtesy, the sincere sympathy, the smiling friendship, that people profess. The whole of these masks as a rule are merely, as I have said, a disguise for some industry, commerce, or speculation. It is merchants alone who in this respect constitute any honest class. They are the only people who give themselves out to be what they are and therefore they go about without any mask at all, and consequently take a humble rank.

It is very necessary that a man should be apprised early in life that it is a masquerade in which he finds himself. For otherwise there are many things which he will fail to understand and put up with, nay, at which he will be completely puzzled, and that man longest of all whose heart is made of better clay—

Et meliore luto finxit praecordia Titan.{1}

{Footnote 1: Juvenal, Sat. 14, 34}

Such for instance is the favour that villainy finds; the neglect that merit, even the rarest and the greatest, suffers at the hands of those of the same profession; the hatred of truth and great capacity; the ignorance of scholars in their own province; and the fact that true wares are almost always despised and the merely specious ones in request. Therefore, let even the young be instructed betimes that in this masquerade the apples are of wax, the flowers of silk, the fish of pasteboard, and that all things—yes, all things—are toys and trifles; and that of two men whom he may see earnestly engaged in business, one is supplying spurious goods and the other paying for them in false coin.

But there are more serious reflections to be made, and worse things to be recorded. Man is at bottom a savage, horrible beast. We know it, if only in the business of taming and restraining him which we call civilization. Hence it is that we are terrified if now and then his nature breaks out. Wherever and whenever the locks and chains of law and order fall off and give place to anarchy, he shows himself for what he is. But it is unnecessary to wait for anarchy in order to gain enlightenment on this subject. A hundred records, old and new, produce the conviction that in his unrelenting cruelty man is in no way inferior to the tiger and the hyaena. A forcible example is supplied by a publication of the year 1841 entitled Slavery and the Internal Slave Trade in the United States of North America: being replies to questions transmitted by the British Anti-slavery Society to the American Anti-slavery Society.{1} This book constitutes one of the heaviest indictments against the human race. No one can put it down with a feeling of horror, and few without tears. For whatever the reader may have ever heard, or imagined, or dreamt, of the unhappy condition of slavery, or indeed of human cruelty in general, it will seem small to him when he reads of the way in which those devils in human form, those bigoted, church-going, strictly Sabbatarian rascals— and in particular the Anglican priests among them—treated their innocent black brothers, who by wrong and violence had got into their diabolical clutches.

{Footnote 1: Translator's 'Note.—If Schopenhauer were writing today, he would with equal truth point to the miseries of the African trade. I have slightly abridged this passage, as some of the evils against which he protested no longer exist.}

Other examples are furnished by Tshudi's Travels in Peru, in the description which he gives of the treatment of the Peruvian soldiers at the hands of their officers; and by Macleod's Travels in Eastern Africa, where the author tells of the cold-blooded and truly devilish cruelty with which the Portuguese in Mozambique treat their slaves. But we need not go for examples to the New World, that obverse side of our planet. In the year 1848 it was brought to life that in England, not in one, but apparently in a hundred cases within a brief period, a husband had poisoned his wife or vice versâ or both had joined in poisoning their children, or in torturing them slowly to death by starving and ill-treating them, with no other object than to get the money for burying them which they had insured in the Burial Clubs against their death. For this purpose, a child was often insured in several, even in as many as twenty clubs at once.{1}

{Footnote 1: Cf. The Times, 20th, 22nd and 23rd Sept. 1848, and also 12th Dec. 1853.}

Details of this character belong, indeed, to the blackest pages in the criminal records of humanity. But, when all is said, it is the inward and innate character of man, this god par excellence of the Pantheists, from which they and everything like them proceed. In every man their dwells, first and foremost, a colossal egoism, which breaks the bounds of right and justice with the greatest freedom, as everyday life shows on a small scale and as history on every page of it on a large. Does not the recognized need of a balance of power in Europe, with the anxious way in which it is preserved, demonstrate that man is a beast of prey, who no sooner sees a weaker man near him than he falls upon him without fail? and does not the same hold good of the affairs of ordinary life?

But to the boundless egoism of our nature there is joined more or less in every human breast a fund of hatred, anger, envy, rancour, and malice, accumulated like the venom in a serpent's tooth, and waiting only for an opportunity of venting itself, and then, like a demon unchained, of storming and raging. If a man has no great occasion for breaking out, he will end by taking advantage of the smallest, and by working it up into something great by the aid of his imagination; for, however small it may be, it is enough to rouse his anger—

Quantulacunque adeo est occasio, sufficit irae{1}—
{Footnote 1: Juvenal, Sat. 13, 183.}

and then he will carry it as far as he can and may. We see this in daily life, where such outbursts are well known under the name of "venting one's gall on something." It will also have been observed that if such outbursts meet with no opposition the subject of them feels decidedly the better for them afterwards. That anger is not without its pleasure is a truth that was recorded even by Aristotle;{1} and he quotes a passage from Homer, who declares anger to be sweeter than honey. But not in anger alone—in hatred too, which stands to anger like a chronic to an acute disease, a man may indulge with the greatest delight:

{Footnote 1: Rhet., i., 11; ii., 2.}

> *Now hatred is by far the longest pleasure,*
> *Men love in haste, but they detest at leisure{1}*

{Footnote 1: Byron Don Juan, c. xiii, 6.}

Gobineau in his work Les Races Humaines has called man l'animal méchant par excellence. People take this very ill, because they feel that it hits them; but he is quite right, for man is the only animal which causes pain to others without any further purpose than just to cause it. Other animals never do it except to satisfy their hunger, or in the rage of combat. If it is said against the tiger that he kills more than eats, he strangles his prey only for the purpose of eating it; and if he cannot eat it, the only explanation is, as the French phrase has it, that ses yeux sont plus grands que son estomac. No animal ever torments another for the mere purpose of tormenting, but man does it and it is this that constitutes the diabolical feature in his character which is so much worse than the merely animal. I have already spoken of the matter in its broad aspect; but it is manifest even in small things, and every reader has a daily opportunity of observing it. For instance, if two little dogs are playing together—and what a genial and charming sight it is—

and a child of three or four years joins them, it is almost inevitable for it to begin hitting them with a whip or stick, and thereby show itself, even at that age, l'animal méchant par excellence. The love of teasing and playing tricks, which is common enough, may be traced to the same source. For instance, if a man has expressed his annoyance at any interruption or other petty inconvenience, there will be no lack of people who for that very reason will bring it about: animal méchant par excellence! This is so certain that a man should be careful not to express any annoyance at small evils. On the other hand, he should also be careful not to express his pleasure at any trifle, for, if he does so, men will act like the jailer who, when he found that his prisoner had performed the laborious task of taming a spider, and took a pleasure in watching it, immediately crushed it under his foot: l'animal méchant par excellence! This is why all animals are instinctively afraid of the sight, or even of the track of a man, that animal méchant par excellence! nor does their instinct them false; for it is man alone who hunts game for which he has no use, and which does him no harm.

It is a fact, then, that in the heart of every man there lies a wild beast which only waits for an opportunity to storm and rage, in its desire to inflict pain on others, or, if they stand in his way, to kill them. It is this which is the source of all the lust of war and battle. In trying to tame and to some extent hold it in check, the intelligence, its appointed keeper, has always enough to do. People may, if they please, call it the radical evil of human nature—a name which will at least serve those with whom a word stands for an explanation. I say, however, that it is the will to live, which, more and more embittered by the constant sufferings of existence, seeks to alleviate its own torment by causing torment in others. But in this way a man gradually develops in himself real cruelty and malice. The observation may also be added that as, according to Kant, matter subsists only through the antagonism of the powers of expansion and contraction, so human society subsists only by the antagonism of hatred, or anger, and fear. For there is a moment in the life of all of us when the malignity of our nature might perhaps make us murderers, if it were not accompanied by a due admixture of fear to keep it within bounds; and this fear, again, would make a man the sport and laughingstock of every boy, if anger were not lying ready in him, and keeping watch.

But it is Schadenfreude, a mischievous delight in the misfortunes of others, which remains the worst trait in human nature. It is a feeling which is closely akin to cruelty, and differs from it, to say the truth, only as theory from practice. In general, it may be said of it that it takes the place which pity ought to take—pity which is its opposite, and the true source of all real justice and charity.

Envy is also opposed to pity, but in another sense; envy, that is to say, is produced by a cause directly antagonistic to that which produces the delight in mischief. The opposition between pity and envy on the one hand, and pity and the delight in mischief on the other, rests, in the main, on the occasions which call them forth. In the case of envy, it is only as a direct effect of the cause which excites it that we feel it at all. That is just the reason why envy, although it is a reprehensible feeling, still admits of some excuse, and is, in general, a very human quality; whereas the delight in mischief is diabolical, and its taunts are the laughter of hell.

The delight in mischief, as I have said, takes the place which pity ought to take. Envy, on the contrary, finds a place only where there is no inducement to pity, or rather an inducement to its opposite; and it is just as this opposite that envy arises in the human breast; and so far, therefore, it may still be reckoned a human sentiment. Nay, I am afraid that no one will be found to be entirely free from it. For that a man should feel his own lack of things more bitterly at the sight of another's delight in the enjoyment of them, is natural; nay, it is inevitable; but this should not rouse his hatred of the man who is happier than himself. It is just this hatred, however, in which true envy consists of. Least of all should a man be envious, when it is a question, not of the gifts of fortune, or chance, or another's favour, but of the gifts of nature; because everything that is innate in a man rest on a metaphysical basis and possesses justification of a higher kind; it is, so to speak, given him by Divine grace. But unhappily, it is just in the case of personal advantages that envy is most irreconcilable. Thus, it is that intelligence, or even genius, cannot get on in the world without begging pardon for its existence, wherever it is not in a position to be able, proudly, and boldly, to despise the world.

In other words, if envy is aroused only by wealth, rank, or power, it is often kept down by egoism, which perceives that, on occasion, assistance, enjoyment, support, protection, advancement, and so on, may be hoped for from the object of envy or that at least by intercourse with him a man may himself win honour from the reflected light of his superiority; and here, too, there is the hope of one day attaining all those advantages himself. On the other hand, in the envy that is directed to natural gifts and personal advantages, like beauty in women or intelligence in men, there is no consolation or hope of one kind or the other; so that nothing remains but to indulge a bitter and irreconcilable hatred of the person who possesses these privileges; and hence the only remaining desire is to take vengeance on him.

But here the envious man finds himself in an unfortunate position; for all his blows fall powerless as soon as it is known that they come from him. Accordingly, he hides his feelings as carefully as if they were secret sins and so becomes an inexhaustible inventor of tricks and artifices and devices for concealing and masking his procedure, in order that, unperceived, he may wound the object of his envy. For instance, with an air of the utmost unconcern he will ignore the advantages which are eating his heart out; he will neither see them, nor know them, nor have observed or even heard of them and thus make himself a master in the art of dissimulation. With great cunning he will completely overlook the man whose brilliant qualities are gnawing at his heart, and act as though he were quite an unimportant person; he will take no notice of him, and, on occasion, will have even quite forgotten his existence. But at the same time, he will before all things endeavour by secret machination carefully to deprive those advantages of any opportunity of showing themselves and becoming known. Then out of his dark corner he will attack these qualities with censure, mockery, ridicule, and calumny, like the toad which spurts its poison from a hole. No less will he enthusiastically praise unimportant people, or even indifferent or bad performances in the same sphere. In short, he will become a Proteas in stratagem, in order to wound others without showing himself. But what is the use of it? The trained eye recognizes him in spite of it all. He betrays himself, if by nothing else, by the way in which he timidly avoids and flies from the object of his envy, who stands the more completely alone, the more brilliant he is; and this is the reason why pretty girls have no friends of their own sex. He betrays himself, too, by the causeless hatred which he shows—a hatred which finds vent in a violent explosion at any circumstance however trivial, though it is often only the product of his imagination. How many such men there are in the world may be recognized by the universal praise of modesty, that is, of a virtue invented on behalf of dull and commonplace people. Nevertheless, it is a virtue which, by exhibiting the necessity for dealing considerately with the wretched plight of these people, is just what calls attention to it.

For our self-consciousness and our pride there can be nothing more flattering than the sight of envy lurking in its retreat and plotting its schemes but never let a man forget that where there is envy there is hatred and let him be careful not to make a false friend out of any envious person. Therefore, it is important to our safety to lay envy bare; and a man should study to discover its tricks, as it is everywhere to be found and always goes about incognito; or as I have said, like a venomous toad it lurks in dark corners. It deserves neither quarter nor sympathy; but as we can never reconcile it let our rule of conduct be to scorn it with a good heart and as our happiness and glory is torture to it, we may rejoice in its sufferings:

> *Den Neid wirst nimmer du versöhnen;*
> *So magst du ihn getrost verhöhnen.*
> *Dein Glück, dein Ruhm ist ihm ein Leiden:*
> *Magst drum a seiner Quaal dich weiden.*

We have been taking a look at the depravity of man, and it is a sight which may well fill us with horror. But now we must cast our eyes on the misery of his existence; and when we have done so, and are horrified by that too, we must look back again at his depravity. We shall then find that they hold the balance to each other. We shall perceive the eternal justice of things; for we shall recognize that the world is itself the Last Judgment on it, and we shall begin to understand why it is that everything that lives must pay the penalty of its existence, first in living and then in dying. Thus, the evil of the penalty accords with the evil of the sin—malum poenae with malum culpae. From the same point of view, we lose our indignation at that intellectual incapacity of the great majority of mankind which in life so often disgusts us. In this Sansara, as the Buddhists call it, human misery, human depravity, and human folly correspond with one another perfectly, and they are of like magnitude. But if, on some special inducement, we direct our gaze to one of them, and survey it in particular, it seems to exceed the other two. This, however, is an illusion and merely the effect of their colossal range.

All things proclaim this Sansara; more than all else, the world of mankind; in which, from a moral point of view, villainy, and baseness and from an intellectual point of view, incapacity, and stupidity, prevail to a horrifying extent. Nevertheless, there appear in it, although very spasmodically, and always as a fresh surprise, manifestations of honesty, of goodness, nay, even of nobility and also of great intelligence, of the thinking mind of genius. They never quite vanish, but like single points of light gleam upon us out of the great dark mass. We must accept them as a pledge that this Sansara contains a good and redeeming principle, which is capable of breaking through and of filling and freeing the whole of it.

The readers of my Ethics know that with me the ultimate foundation of morality is the truth which in the Vedas and the Vedanta receives its expression in the established, mystical formula, Tat twam asi (This is thyself), which is spoken with reference to every living thing, be it man or beast, and is called the Mahavakya, the great word.

Actions which proceed in accordance with this principle, such as those of the philanthropist, may indeed be regarded as the beginning of mysticism. Every benefit rendered with a pure intention proclaims that the man who exercises it acts in direct conflict with the world of appearance; for he recognizes himself as identical with another individual, who exists in complete separation from him. Accordingly, all disinterested kindness is inexplicable; it is a mystery; and hence in order to explain it a man has to resort to all sorts of fictions. When Kant had demolished all other arguments for theism, he admitted one only, that it gave the best interpretation and solution of such mysterious actions, and of all others like them. He therefore allowed it to stand as a presumption unsusceptible indeed of theoretical proof, but valid from a practical point of view. I may, however, express my doubts whether he was quite serious about it. For to make morality rest on theism is really to reduce morality to egoism; although the English, it is true, as also the lowest classes of society with us, do not perceive the possibility of any other foundation for it.

The above-mentioned recognition of a man's own true being in another individual objectively presented to him, is exhibited in a particularly beautiful and clear way in the cases in which a man, already destined to death beyond any hope of rescue, gives himself up to the welfare of others with great solicitude and zeal, and tries to save them. Of this kind is the well-known story of a servant who was bitten in a courtyard at night by a mad dog. In the belief that she was beyond hope, she seized the dog and dragged it into a stable, which she then locked, so that no one else might be bitten. Then again there is the incident in Naples, which Tischbein has immortalized in one of his aquarelles. A son, fleeing from the lava, which is rapidly streaming toward the sea, is carrying his aged father on his back. When there is only a narrow strip of land left between the devouring elements, the father bids the son put him down, so that the son may save himself by flight, as otherwise both will be lost. The son obeys and as he goes casts a glance of farewell on his father. This is the moment depicted. The historical circumstance which Scott represents in his masterly way in The Heart of Midlothian, chap, ii., is of a precisely similar kind; where, of two delinquents condemned to death, the one who by his awkwardness caused the capture of the other happily sets him free in the chapel by overpowering the guard after the execution-sermon, without at the same time making any attempt on his own behalf. Nay, in the same category must also be placed the scene, which is represented in a common engraving, which may perhaps be objectionable to western readers—I mean the one in which a soldier, kneeling to be shot, is trying by waving a cloth to frighten away his dog who wants to come to him.

In all these cases we see an individual in the face of his own immediate and certain destruction no longer thinking of saving himself, so that he may direct the whole of his efforts to saving someone else. How could there be a clearer expression of the consciousness that what is being destroyed is only a phenomenon and that the destruction itself is only a phenomenon; that, on the other hand, the real being of the man who meets his death is untouched by that event, and lives on in the other man, in whom even now, as his action betrays, he so clearly perceives it to exist?

For if this were not so, and it was his real being which was about to be annihilated, how could that being spend its last efforts in showing such an ardent sympathy in the welfare and continued existence of another?

There are two different ways in which a man may become conscious of his own existence. On the one hand, he may have an empirical perception of it, as it manifests itself externally—something so small that it approaches vanishing point; set in a world which, as regards time and space, is infinite; one only of the thousand millions of human creatures who run about on this planet for a very brief period and are renewed every thirty years. On the other hand, by going down into the depths of his own nature, a man may become conscious that he is all in all; that, in fact, he is the only real being; and that, in addition, this real being perceives itself again in others, who present themselves from without, as though they formed a mirror of himself.

Of these two ways in which a man may come to know what he is, the first grasps the phenomenon alone, the mere product of the principle of individuation; whereas the second makes a man immediately conscious that he is the thing-in-itself. This is a doctrine in which, as regards the first way, I have Kant, and as regards both, I have the Vedas, to support me.

There is, it is true, a simple objection to the second method. It may be said to assume that one and the same being can exist in different places at the same time, and yet be complete in each of them. Although, from an empirical point of view, this is the most palpable impossibility—nay, absurdity—it is nevertheless perfectly true of the thing-in-itself. The impossibility and the absurdity of it, empirically, are only due to the forms which phenomena assume, in accordance with the principle of individuation. For the thing-in-itself, the will to live, exists whole and undivided in every being, even in the smallest, as completely as in the sum-total of all things that ever were or are or will be. This is why every being, even the smallest, says to itself, So long as I am safe, let the world perish—dum ego salvus sim, pereat mundus. And, in truth, even if only one individual were left in the world, and all the rest were to perish, the one that remained would still possess the whole self-being of the world, uninjured and undiminished, and would laugh at the destruction of the world as an illusion. This conclusion per impossible may be balanced by the counter-conclusion, which is on all fours with it, that if that last individual were to be annihilated in and with him the whole world would be destroyed. It was in this sense that the mystic Angelas Silesius{1} declared that God could not live for a moment without him, and that if he were to be annihilated God must of necessity give up the ghost:

> *Ich weiss dass ohne mich Gott nicht ein Nu kann leben;*
>
> *Werd' ich zunicht, er muss von Noth den Geist aufgeben.*

{Footnote 1: Translator's Note.—Angelus Silesius, see Counsels and Maxims, p. 39, note.}

But the empirical point of view also to some extent enables us to perceive that it is true, or at least possible, that our self can exist in other beings whose consciousness is separated and different from our own. That this is, so is shown by the experience of somnambulists. Although the identity of their ego is preserved throughout, they know nothing, when they awake, of all that a moment before they themselves said, did or suffered. So entirely is the individual consciousness a phenomenon that even in the same ego two consciousnesses can arise of which the one knows nothing of the other.

GOVERNMENT.

It is a characteristic failing of the Germans to look in the clouds for what lies at their feet. An excellent example of this is furnished by the treatment which the idea of Natural Right has received at the hands of professors of philosophy. When they are called upon to explain those simple relations of human life which make up the substance of this right, such as Right and Wrong, Property, State, Punishment and so on, they have recourse to the most extravagant, abstract, remote and meaningless conceptions, and out of them build a Tower of Babel reaching to the clouds, and taking this or that form according to the special whim of the professor for the time being. The clearest and simplest relations of life, such as affect us directly, are thus made quite unintelligible, to the great detriment of the young people who are educated in such a school. These relations themselves are perfectly simple and easily understood—as the reader may convince himself if he will turn to the account which I have given of them in the Foundation of Morality, § 17, and in my chief work, bk. i., § 62. But at the sound of certain words, like Right, Freedom, the Good, Being—this nugatory infinitive of the cupola—and many others of the same sort, the German's head begins to swim, and falling straightway into a kind of delirium he launches forth into high-flown phrases which have no meaning whatever. He takes the most remote and empty conceptions, and strings them together artificially, instead of fixing his eyes on the facts, and looking at things and relations as they really are. It is these things and relations which supply the ideas of Right and Freedom and give them the only true meaning that they possess.

The man who starts from the preconceived opinion that the conception of Right must be a positive one, and then attempts to define it, will fail; for he is trying to grasp a shadow, to pursue a spectre, to search for what does not exist. The conception of Right is a negative one, like the conception of Freedom; its content is mere negation. It is the conception of Wrong which is positive; Wrong has the same significance as injury—laesio—in the widest sense of the term. An injury may be done either to a man's person or to his property or to his honour and accordingly a man's rights are easy to define everyone has a right to do anything that injures no one else.

To have a right to do or claim a thing means nothing more than to be able to do or take or vise it without thereby injuring anyone else. Simplex sigillum veri. This definition shows how senseless many questions are; for instance, the question whether we have the right to take our own life, As far as concerns the personal claims which others may possibly have upon us, they are subject to the condition that we are alive and fall to the ground when we die. To demand of a man, who does not care to live any longer for himself, that he should live on as a mere machine for the advantage of others is an extravagant pretension.

Although men's powers differ, their rights are alike. Their rights do not rest upon their powers, because Right is of a moral complexion; they rest on the fact that the same will to live shows itself in every man at the same stage of its manifestation. This, however, only applies to that original and abstract Right, which a man possesses as a man. The property, and also the honour, which a man acquires for himself by the exercise of his powers, depend on the measure and kind of power which he possesses, and so lend his Right a wider sphere of application. Here, then, equality comes to an end. The man who is better equipped, or more active, increases by adding to his gains, not his Right, but the number of the things to which it extends.

In my chief work{1} I have proved that the State in its essence is merely an institution existing for the purpose of protecting its members against outward attack or inward dissension. It follows from this that the ultimate ground on which the State is necessary is the acknowledged lack of Right in the human race. If Right were there, no one would think of a State; for no one would have any fear that his rights would be impaired and a mere union against the attacks of wild beasts or the elements would have very little analogy with what we mean by a State. From this point of view, it is easy to see how dull and stupid are the philosophasters who in pompous phrases represent that the State is the supreme end and flower of human existence. Such a view is the apotheosis of Philistinism.

{Footnote 1: 1 Bk. ii., ch. xlvii.}

If it were Right that ruled in the world, a man would have done enough in building his house and would need no other protection than the right of possessing it, which would be obvious. But since Wrong is the order of the day, it is requisite that the man who has built his house should also be able to protect it. Otherwise, his Right is de facto incomplete; the aggressor, that is to say, has the right of might—Faustrecht; and this is just the conception of Right which Spinoza entertains. He recognises no other. His words are: unusquisque tantum juris habet quantum potentia valet;{1} each man has as much right as he has power. And again: uniuscujusque jus potentia ejus definitur; each man's right is determined by his power.{2} Hobbes seems to have started this conception of Right,{3} and he adds the strange comment that the Right of the good Lord to all things rests on nothing but His omnipotence.

{Footnote 1: Tract. Theol. Pol., ch. ii., § 8.}

{Footnote 2: Ethics, IV., xxxvii., 1.}

{Footnote 3: Particularly in a passage in the De Cive, I, § 14.}

Now this is a conception of Right which, both in theory and in practice, no longer prevails in the civic world; but in the world in general, though abolished in theory, it continues to apply in practice. The consequences of neglecting it may be seen in the case of China. Threatened by rebellion within and foes without, this great empire is in a defenceless state and has to pay the penalty of having cultivated only the arts of peace and ignored the arts of war.

There is a certain analogy between the operations of nature and those of man, which is a peculiar but not fortuitous character, and is based on the identity of the will in both. When the herbivorous animals had taken their place in the organic world, beasts of prey made their appearance—necessarily a late appearance—in each species and proceeded to live upon them. Just in the same way, as soon as by honest toil and in the sweat of their faces men have won from the ground what is needed for the support of their societies, a number of individuals are sure to arise in some of these societies, who, instead of cultivating the earth and living on its produce, prefer to take their lives in their hands and risk health and freedom by falling upon those who are in possession of what they have honestly earned, and by appropriating the fruits of their labour. These are the beasts of prey in the human race; they are the conquering peoples whom we find everywhere in history, from the most ancient to the most recent times. Their varying fortunes, as at one moment they succeed and at another fail, make up the general elements of the history of the world. Hence Voltaire was perfectly right when he said that the aim of all war is robbery. That those who engage in it are ashamed of their doings is clear by the fact that governments loudly protest their reluctance to appeal to arms except for purposes of self-defence. Instead of trying to excuse themselves by telling public and official lies, which are almost more revolting than war itself, they should take their stand, as bold as brass, on Macchiavelli's doctrine. The gist of it may be stated to be this: that whereas between one individual and another, and so far as concerns the law and morality of their relations, the principle, Don't do to others what you wouldn't like done to yourself, certainly applies, it is the converse of this principle which is appropriate in the case of nations and in politics: What you wouldn't like done to yourself do to others. If you do not want to be put under a foreign yoke, take time by the forelock, and put your neighbour under it himself; whenever, that is to say, his weakness offers you the opportunity. For if you let the opportunity pass, it will desert one day to the enemy's camp and offer itself there. Then your enemy will put you under his yoke; and your failure to grasp the opportunity may be paid for, not by the generation, which was guilty of it, but by the next. This Macchiavellian principle is always a much more decent cloak for the lust of robbery than the rags of very obvious lies in a speech from the head of the State; lies, too, of a description which recalls the well-known story of the rabbit attacking the dog. Every State looks upon its neighbours as at bottom a horde of robbers, who will fall upon it as soon as they have the opportunity.

Between the serf, the farmer, the tenant, and the mortgagee, the difference is rather one of form than of substance. Whether the peasant belongs to me, or the land on which he has to get a living; whether the bird is mine, or its food, the tree, or its fruit, is a matter of little moment; for, as Shakespeare makes Shylock say:

You take my life When you do take the means whereby, I live.

The free peasant has, indeed, the advantage that he can go off and seek his fortune in the wide world; whereas the serf who is attached to the soil, glebae adscriptus, has an advantage which is perhaps still greater, that when failure of crops or illness, old age or incapacity, render him helpless, his master must look after him, and so he sleeps well at night; whereas, if the crops fail, his master tosses about on his bed trying to think how he is to procure bread for his men. As long ago as Menander it was said that it is better to be the slave of a good master than to live miserably as a freeman. Another advantage possessed by the free is that if they have any talents, they can improve their position; but the same advantage is not wholly withheld from the slave. If he proves himself useful to his master by the exercise of any skill, he is treated; accordingly, just as in ancient Rome mechanics, foremen of workshops, architects, nay, even doctors, were generally slaves.

Slavery and poverty, then, are only two forms, I might almost say only two names of the same thing, the essence of which is that a man's physical powers are employed, in the main, not for himself but for others; and this leads partly to his being over-loaded with work, and partly to his getting a scanty satisfaction for his needs. For Nature has given a man only as much physical power as will suffice, if he exerts it in moderation, to gain a sustenance from the earth. No great superfluity of power is his. If then, a not inconsiderable number of men are relieved from the common burden of sustaining the existence of the human race, the burden of the remainder is augmented, and they suffer. This is the chief source of the evil which under the name of slavery, or under the name of the proletariat, has always oppressed the great majority of the human race.

But the more remote cause of it is luxury. In order, it may be said, that some few persons may have what is unnecessary, superfluous, and the product of refinement—nay, in order that they may satisfy artificial needs—a great part of the existing powers of mankind has to be devoted to this object and therefore withdrawn from the production of what is necessary and indispensable. Instead of building cottages for themselves, thousands of men build mansions for a few. Instead of weaving coarse materials for themselves and their families, they make fine cloths, silk, or even lace, for the rich, and in general manufacture a thousand objects of luxury for their pleasure. A great part of the urban population consists of workmen who make these articles of luxury; and for them and those who give them work the peasants have to plough and sow and look after the flocks as well as for themselves, and thus have more labour than Nature originally imposed upon them. Moreover, the urban population devotes a great deal of physical strength, and a great deal of land, to such things as wine, silk, tobacco, hops, asparagus and so on, instead of to corn, potatoes, and cattle-breeding. Further, a number of men are withdrawn from agriculture and employed in shipbuilding and seafaring, in order that sugar, coffee, tea and other goods may be imported. In short, a large part of the powers of the human race is taken away from the production of what is necessary, in order to bring what is superfluous and unnecessary within the reach of a few. As long therefore as luxury exists, there must be a corresponding amount of over-work and misery, whether it takes the name of poverty or of slavery. The fundamental difference between the two is that slavery originates in violence, and poverty in craft. The whole unnatural condition of society—the universal struggle to escape from misery, the sea-trade attended with so much loss of life, the complicated interests of commerce, and finally the wars to which it all gives rise—is due, only and alone, to luxury, which gives no happiness even to those who enjoy it, nay, makes them ill and bad tempered. Accordingly, it looks as if the most effective way of alleviating human misery would be to diminish luxury, or even abolish it altogether.

There is unquestionably much truth in this train of thought. But the conclusion at which it arrives is refuted by an argument possessing this advantage over it—that it is confirmed by the testimony of experience. A certain amount of work is devoted to purposes of luxury. What the human race loses in this way in the muscular power which would otherwise be available for the necessities of existence is gradually made up to it a thousandfold by the nervous power, which, in a chemical sense, is thereby released. And since the intelligence and sensibility which are thus promoted are on a higher level than the muscular irritability which they supplant, so the achievements of mind exceed those of the body a thousandfold. One wise counsel is worth the work of many hands:

{Greek: Hos en sophon bouleuma tas pollon cheiras nika.}

A nation of nothing but peasants would do little in the way of discovery and invention; but idle hands make active heads. Science and the Arts are themselves the children of luxury, and they discharge their debt to it. The work which they do is to perfect technology in all its branches, mechanical, chemical, and physical; an art which in our days has brought machinery to a pitch never dreamt of before, and in particular has, by steam and electricity, accomplished things the like of which would, in earlier ages, have been ascribed to the agency of the devil. In manufactures of all kinds, and to some extent in agriculture, machines now do a thousand times more than could ever have been done by the hands of all the well-to-do, educated, and professional classes, and could ever have been attained if all luxury had been abolished and every one had returned to the life of a peasant. It is by no means the rich alone, but all classes, who derive benefit from these industries. Things which in former days hardly anyone could afford are now cheap and abundant, and even the lowest classes are much better off in point of comfort. In the Middle Ages a King of England once borrowed a pair of silk stockings from one of his lords, so that he might wear them in giving an audience to the French ambassador. Even Queen Elizabeth was greatly pleased and astonished to receive a pair as a New Year's present; today every shopman has them. Fifty years ago, ladies wore the kind of calico gowns which servants wear now. If mechanical science continues to progress at the same rate for any length of time, it may end by saving human labour almost entirely, just as horses are even now being largely superseded by machines. For it is possible to conceive that intellectual culture might in some degree become general in the human race; and this would be impossible as long as bodily labour was incumbent on any great part of it. Muscular irritability and nervous sensibility are always and everywhere, both generally and particularly, in antagonism; for the simple reason that it is one and the same vital power which underlies both. Further, since the arts have a softening effect on character, it is possible that quarrels great and small, wars and duels, will vanish from the world; just as both have become much rarer occurrences. However, it is not my object here to write a Utopia.

But apart from all this the arguments used above in favour of the abolition of luxury and the uniform distribution of all bodily labour are open to the objection that the great mass of mankind, always and everywhere, cannot do without leaders, guides and counsellors, in one shape or another, according to the matter in question; judges, governors, generals, officials, priests, doctors, men of learning, philosophers, and so on, are all a necessity. Their common task is to lead the race for the greater part so incapable and perverse, through the labyrinth of life, of which each of them according to his position and capacity has obtained a general view, be his range wide or narrow. That these guides of the race should be permanently relieved of all bodily labour as well as of all vulgar need and discomfort; nay, that in proportion to their much greater achievements they should necessarily own and enjoy more than the common man, is natural and reasonable. Great merchants should also be included in the same privileged class, whenever they make far-sighted preparations for national needs.

The question of the sovereignty of the people is at bottom the same as the question whether any man can have an original right to rule a people against its will. How that proposition can be reasonably maintained I do not see. The people, it must be admitted, is sovereign; but it is a sovereign who is always a minor. It must have permanent guardians, and it can never exercise its rights itself, without creating dangers of which no one can foresee the end; especially as like all minors, it is very apt to become the sport of designing sharpers, in the shape of what are called demagogues.

Voltaire remarks that the first man to become a king was a successful soldier. It is certainly the case that all princes were originally victorious leaders of armies, and for a long time it was as such that they bore sway. On the rise of standing armies' princes began to regard their people as a means of sustaining themselves and their soldiers and treated them, accordingly, as though they were a herd of cattle, which had to be tended in order that it might provide wool, milk, and meat. The why and wherefore of all this, as I shall presently show in detail, is the fact that originally it was not right, but might, that ruled in the world. Might has the advantage of having been the first in the field. That is why it is impossible to do away with it and abolish it altogether; it must always have its place; and all that a man can wish or ask is that it should be found on the side of right and associated with it. Accordingly says the prince to his subjects: "I rule you in virtue of the power which I possess. But, on the other hand, it excludes that of anyone else and I shall suffer none but my own, whether it comes from without, or arises within by one of you trying to oppress another. In this way, then, you are protected." The arrangement was carried out; and just because it was carried out the old idea of kingship developed with time and progress into quite a different idea, and put the other one in the background, where it may still be seen, now and then, flitting about like a spectre. Its place has been taken by the idea of the king as father of his people, as the firm and unshakable pillar which alone supports and maintains the whole organization of law and order, and consequently the rights of every man.{1}

{Footnote 1: We read in Stobaeus, Florilegium, ch. xliv., 41, of a Persian custom, by which, whenever a king died, there was a five days' anarchy, in order that people might perceive the advantage of having kings and laws.}

But a king can accomplish this only by inborn prerogative which reserves authority to him and to him alone—an authority which is supreme, indubitable, and beyond all attack, nay, to which everyone renders instinctive obedience. Hence the king is rightly said to rule "by the grace of God." He is always the most useful person in the State, and his services are never too dearly repaid by any Civil List, however heavy.

But even as late a writer as Macchiavelli was so decidedly imbued with the earlier or mediaeval conception of the position of a prince that he treats it as a matter which is self-evident: he never discusses it, but tacitly takes it as the presupposition and basis of his advice. It may be said generally that his book is merely the theoretical statement and consistent and systematic exposition of the practice prevailing in his time. It is the novel statement of it in a complete theoretical form that lends it such a poignant interest. The same thing, I may remark in passing, applies to the immortal little work of La Rochefaucauld, who, however, takes private and not public life for his theme, and offers, not advice, but observations. The title of this fine little book is open, perhaps, to some objection: the contents are not, as a rule, either maxims or reflections, but aperçus; and that is what they should be called. There is much, too, in Macchiavelli that will be found also to apply to private life.

Right in itself is powerless; in nature it is Might that rules. To enlist might on the side of right, so that by means of it right may rule, is the problem of statesmanship. And it is indeed a hard problem, as will be obvious if we remember that almost every human breast is the seat of an egoism which has no limits and is usually associated with an accumulated store of hatred and malice; so that at the very start feelings of enmity largely prevail over those of friendship. We have also to bear in mind that it is many millions of individuals so constituted who have to be kept in the bonds of law and order, peace, and tranquility; whereas originally everyone had a right to say to everyone else: I am just as good as you are! A consideration of all this must fill us with surprise that on the whole the world pursues its way so peacefully and quietly, and with so much law and order as we see to exist. It is the machinery of State which alone accomplishes it. For it is physical power alone which has any direct action on men; constituted as they generally are, it is for physical power alone that they have any feeling or respect.

If a man would convince himself by experience that this is the case, he need do nothing but remove all compulsion from his fellows and try to govern them by clearly and forcibly representing to them what is reasonable, right, and fair, though at the same time it may be contrary to their interests. He would be laughed to scorn; and as things go that is the only answer he would get. It would soon be obvious to him that moral force alone is powerless. It is, then, physical force alone which is capable of securing respect. Now this force ultimately resides in the masses, where it is associated with ignorance, stupidity, and injustice. Accordingly, the main aim of statesmanship in these difficult circumstances is to put physical force in subjection to mental force—to intellectual superiority and thus to make it serviceable. But if this aim is not itself accompanied by justice and good intentions the result of the business, if it succeeds, is that the State so erected consists of knaves and fools, the deceivers and the deceived. That this is the case is made gradually evident by the progress of intelligence amongst the masses, however much it may be repressed; and it leads to revolution. But if, contrarily, intelligence is accompanied by justice and good intentions, there arises a State as perfect as the character of human affairs will allow. It is very much to the purpose if justice and good intentions not only exist, but are also demonstrable and openly exhibited, and can be called to account publicly, and be subject to control. Care must be taken, however, lest the resulting participation of many persons in the work of government should affect the unity of the State and inflict a loss of strength and concentration on the power by which its home and foreign affairs have to be administered. This is what almost always happens in republics. To produce a constitution which should satisfy all these demands would accordingly be the highest aim of statesmanship. But, as a matter of fact, statesmanship has to consider other things as well. It has to reckon with the people as they exist, and their national peculiarities. This is the raw material on which it has to work, and the ingredients of that material will always exercise a great effect on the completed scheme.

Statesmanship will have achieved a good deal if it so far attains its object as to reduce wrong and injustice in the community to a minimum. To banish them altogether, and to leave no trace of them, is merely the ideal to be aimed at; and it is only approximately that it can be reached. If they disappear in one direction, they creep in again in another; for wrong and injustice lie deeply rooted in human nature. Attempts have been made to attain the desired aim by artificial constitutions and systematic codes of law; but they are not in complete touch with the facts—they remain an asymptote, for the simple reason that hard and fast conceptions never embrace all possible cases and cannot be made to meet individual instances. Such conceptions resemble the stones of a mosaic rather than the delicate shading in a picture. Nay, more: all experiments in this matter are attended with danger; because the material in question, namely, the human race, is the most difficult of all material to handle. It is almost as dangerous as an explosive.

No doubt it is true that in the machinery of the State the freedom of the press performs the same function as a safety-valve in other machinery; for it enables all discontent to find a voice; nay, in doing so, the discontent exhausts itself if it has not much substance; and if it has, there is an advantage in recognizing it betimes and applying the remedy. This is much better than to repress the discontent and let it simmer and ferment and go on increasing until it ends in an explosion. On the other hand, the freedom of the press may be regarded as a permission to sell poison—poison for the heart and the mind. There is no idea so foolish but that it cannot be put into the heads of the ignorant and incapable multitude, especially if the idea holds out some prospect of any gain or advantage. And when a man has got hold of any such idea what is there that he will not do? I am, therefore, very much afraid that the danger of a free press outweighs its utility, particularly where the law offers a way of redressing wrongs. In any case, however, the freedom of the press should be governed by a very strict prohibition of all and every anonymity.

Generally, indeed, it may be maintained that right is of a nature analogous to that of certain chemical substances, which cannot be exhibited in a pure and isolated condition, but at the most only with a small admixture of some other substance, which serves as a vehicle for them, or gives them the necessary consistency, such as fluorine or even alcohol, or prussic acid. Pursuing the analogy, we may say that right, if it is to gain a footing in the world and really prevail, must of necessity be supplemented by a small amount of arbitrary force, in order that, notwithstanding its merely ideal and therefore ethereal nature, it may be able to work and subsist in the real and material world, and not evaporate and vanish into the clouds, as it does in Hesoid. Birth-right of every description, all heritable privileges, every form of national religion, and so on, may be regarded as the necessary chemical base or alloy; inasmuch as it is only when right has some such firm and actual foundation that it can be enforced and consistently vindicated. They form for right a sort of {Greek: os moi pou sto}—a fulcrum for supporting its lever.

Linnaeus adopted a vegetable system of an artificial and arbitrary character. It cannot be replaced by a natural one, no matter how reasonable the change might be, or how often it has been attempted to make it, because no other system could ever yield the same certainty and stability of definition. Just in the same way the artificial and arbitrary basis on which, as has been shown, the constitution of a State rests, can never be replaced by a purely natural basis. A natural basis would aim at doing away with the conditions that have been mentioned: in the place of the privileges of birth it would put those of personal merit; in the place of the national religion, the results of rationalistic inquiry, and so on. However agreeable to reason this might all prove; the change could not be made; because a natural basis would lack that certainty and fixity of definition which alone secures the stability of the commonwealth. A constitution which embodied abstract right alone would be an excellent thing for natures other than human, but since the great majority of men are extremely egoistic, unjust, inconsiderate, deceitful and sometimes even malicious; since in addition they are endowed with very scanty intelligence there arises the necessity for a power that shall be concentrated in one man, a power that shall be above all law and right, and be completely irresponsible, nay, to which everything shall yield as to something that is regarded as a creature of a higher kind, a ruler by the grace of God. It is only thus that men can be permanently held in check and governed.

The United States of North America exhibit the attempt to proceed without any such arbitrary basis; that is to say, to allow abstract right to prevail pure and unalloyed. But the result is not attractive. For with all the material prosperity of the country what do we find? The prevailing sentiment is a base Utilitarianism with its inevitable companion, ignorance; and it is this that has paved the way for a union of stupid Anglican bigotry, foolish prejudice, coarse brutality, and a childish veneration of women. Even worse things are the order of the day: most iniquitous oppression of the black freemen, lynch law, frequent assassination often committed with entire impunity, duels of a savagery elsewhere unknown, now and then open scorn of all law and justice, repudiation of public debts, abominable political rascality towards a neighbouring State, followed by a mercenary raid on its rich territory,—afterwards sought to be excused, on the part of the chief authority of the

State, by lies which everyone in the country knew to be such and laughed at—an ever-increasing ochlocracy, and finally all the disastrous influence which this abnegation of justice in high quarters must have exercised on private morals. This specimen of a pure constitution on the obverse side of the planet says very little for republics in general, but still less for the imitations of it in Mexico, Guatemala, Colombia, and Peru.

A peculiar disadvantage attaching to republics—and one that might not be looked for—is that in this form of government it must be more difficult for men of ability to attain high position and exercise direct political influence than in the case of monarchies. For always and everywhere and under all circumstances there is a conspiracy, or instinctive alliance, against such men on the part of all the stupid, the weak, and the commonplace; they look upon such men as their natural enemies, and they are firmly held together by a common fear of them. There is always a numerous host of the stupid and the weak, and in a republican constitution it is easy for them to suppress and exclude the men of ability, so that they may not be outflanked by them. They are fifty to one; and here all have equal rights at the start.

In a monarchy, on the other hand, this natural and universal league of the stupid against those who are possessed of intellectual advantages is a one-sided affair; it exists only from below, for in a monarchy talent and intelligence receive a natural advocacy and support from above. In the first place, the position of the monarch himself is much too high and too firm for him to stand in fear of any sort of competition. In the next place, he serves the State more by his will than by his intelligence; for no intelligence could ever be equal to all the demands that would in his case be made upon it. He is therefore compelled to be always availing himself of other men's intelligence. Seeing that his own interests are securely bound up with those of his country; that they are inseparable from them and one with them, he will naturally give the preference to the best men, because they are his most serviceable instruments, and he will bestow his favour upon them—as soon, that is, as he can find them; which is not so difficult, if only an honest search be made. Just in the same way even ministers of State have too much advantage over rising politicians to need to regard them with jealousy; and accordingly for analogous reasons they are glad to single out distinguished men and set them to work, in order to make use of their powers for themselves. It is in this way that intelligence has always under a monarchical government a much better chance against its irreconcilable and ever-present foe, stupidity; and the advantage which it gains is very great.

In general, the monarchical form of government is that which is natural to man; just as it is natural to bees and ants, to a flight of cranes, a herd of wandering elephants, a pack of wolves seeking prey in common, and many other animals, all of which place one of their number at the head of the business in hand. Every business in which men engage, if it is attended with danger—every campaign, every ship at sea—must also be subject to the authority of one commander; everywhere it is one will that must lead. Even the animal organism is constructed on a monarchical principle: it is the brain alone which guides and governs and exercises the hegemony. Although heart, lungs, and stomach contribute much more to the continued existence of the whole body, these philistines cannot on that account be allowed to guide and lead. That is a business which belongs solely to the brain; government must proceed from one central point. Even the solar system is monarchical. On the other hand, a republic is as unnatural as it is unfavourable to the higher intellectual life and the arts and sciences. Accordingly, we find that everywhere in the world, and at all times, nations, whether civilised or savage, or occupying a position between the two, are always under monarchical government. The rule of many as Homer said, is not a good thing: let there be one ruler, one king.

{Footnote 1: Iliad, ii., 204.}

How would it be possible that, everywhere and at all times, we should see many millions of people, nay, even hundreds of millions, become the willing and obedient subjects of one man, sometimes even one woman, and provisionally, even, of a child, unless there were a monarchical instinct in men which drove them to it as the form of government best suited to them? This arrangement is not the product of reflection. Everywhere one man is king, and for the most part his dignity is hereditary. He is, as it were, the personification, the monogram, of the whole people, which attains an individuality in him. In this sense he can rightly say: l'etat c'est moi. It is precisely for this reason that in Shakespeare's historical plays the kings of England and France mutually address each other as France and England, and the Duke of Austria goes by the name of his country. It is as though the kings regarded themselves as the incarnation of their nationalities. It is all in accordance with human nature; and for this very reason the hereditary monarch cannot separate his own welfare and that of his family from the welfare of his country; as, on the other hand, mostly happens when the monarch is elected, as, for instance, in the States of the Church.{1} The Chinese can conceive of a monarchical government only; what a republic is they utterly fail to understand. When a Dutch legation was in China in the year 1658, it was obliged to represent that the Prince of Orange was their king, as otherwise the Chinese would have been inclined to take Holland for a nest of pirates living without any lord or master. {2} Stobaeus, in a chapter in his Florilegium, at the head of which he wrote That monarchy is best, collected the best of the passages in which the ancients explained the advantages of that form of government. In a word, republics are unnatural and artificial; they are the product of reflection. Hence it is that they occur only as rare exceptions in the whole history of the world. There were the small Greek republics, the Roman and the Carthaginian but they were all rendered possible by the fact that five-sixths, perhaps even seven-eighths, of the population consisted of slaves. In the year 1840, even in the United States, there were three million slaves to a population of sixteen millions. Then, again, the duration of the republics of antiquity, compared with that of monarchies, was very short. Republics are very easy to be found and very difficult to maintain, while with monarchies it is exactly the reverse. If it is Utopian schemes that are wanted, I say this: the only solution of the problem would be a despotism of the wise and the noble, of the true aristocracy and the genuine nobility, brought about by the method of generation—that is, by the marriage of the noblest men with the cleverest and most intellectual women. This is my Utopia, my Republic of Plato.

{Footnote 1: Translator's Note.—The reader will recollect that Schopenhauer was writing long before the Papal territories were absorbed into the kingdom of Italy.}

{Footnote 2: See Jean Nieuhoff, L'Ambassade de la Compagnie Orientale des Provinces Unies vers L'Empereur de la Chine, traduit par Jean le Charpentier à Leyde, 1665; ch. 45.}

Constitutional kings are undoubtedly in much the same position as the gods of Epicurus, who sit upon high in undisturbed bliss and tranquility, and do not meddle with human affairs. Just now they are the fashion. In every German duodecimo-principality a parody of the English constitution is set up, quite complete, from Upper and Lower Houses down to the Habeas Corpus Act and trial by jury. These institutions, which proceed from English character and English circumstances, and presuppose both, are natural and suitable to the English people. It is just as natural to the German people to be split up into a number of different stocks, under a similar number of ruling Princes, with an Emperor over them all, who maintains peace at home, and represents the unity of the State board. It is an arrangement which has proceeded from German character and German circumstances. I am of opinion that if Germany is not to meet with the same fate as Italy, it must restore the imperial crown, which was done away with by its archenemy, the first Napoleon; and it must restore it as effectively as possible. {1} For German unity depends on it, and without the imperial crown it will always be merely nominal, or precarious. But as we no longer live in the days of Günther of Schwarzburg, when the choice of Emperor was a serious business, the imperial crown ought to go alternately to Prussia and to Austria, for the life of the wearer. In any case, the absolute sovereignty of the small States is illusory. Napoleon I. did for Germany what Otto the Great did for Italy: he divided it into small, independent States, on the principle, divide et impera.

{Footnote 1: Translator's Note.—Here, again, it is hardly necessary to say that Schopenhauer, who died in 1860, and wrote this passage at least some years previously, cannot be referring to any of the events which culminated in 1870. The whole passage forms a striking illustration of his political sagacity.}

The English show their great intelligence, amongst other ways, by clinging to their ancient institutions, customs, and usages and by holding them sacred, even at the risk of carrying this tenacity too far and making it ridiculous. They hold them sacred for the simple reason that those institutions and customs are not the invention of an idle head but have grown up gradually by the force of circumstance and the wisdom of life itself and are therefore suited to them as a nation. On the other hand, the German Michel{1} allows himself to be persuaded by his schoolmaster that he must go about in an English dress-coat and that nothing else will do. Accordingly, he has bullied his father into giving it to him and with his awkward manners this ungainly creature presents in it a sufficiently ridiculous figure. But the dress-coat will someday be too tight for him and incommode him. It will not be very long before he feels it in trial by jury. This institution arose in the most barbarous period of the Middle Ages—the times of Alfred the Great, when the ability to read and write exempted a man from the penalty of death. It is the worst of all criminal procedures. Instead of judges, well versed in law and of great experience, who have grown grey in daily unravelling the tricks and wiles of thieves, murderers and rascals of all sorts, and so are well able to get at the bottom of things, it is gossiping tailors and tanners who sit in judgment; it is their coarse, crude, unpracticed and awkward intelligence, incapable of any sustained attention, that is called upon to find out the truth from a tissue of lies and deceit. All the time, moreover, they are thinking of their cloth and their leather, and longing to be at home; and they have absolutely no clear notion at all of the distinction between probability and certainty. It is with this sort of a calculus of probabilities in their stupid heads that they confidently undertake to seal a man's doom.

{Footnote 1: Translator's Note.—It may be well to explain that "Michel" is sometimes used by the Germans as a nickname of their nation, corresponding to "John Bull" as a nickname of the English. Flügel in his German-English Dictionary declares that der deutsche Michel represents the German nation as an honest, blunt, unsuspicious fellow, who easily allows himself to be imposed upon, even, he adds, with a touch of patriotism, "by those who are greatly his inferiors in point of strength and real worth."}

The same remark is applicable to them which Dr. Johnson made of a court-martial in which he had little confidence, summoned to decide a very important case. He said that perhaps there was not a member of it who, in the whole course of his life, had ever spent an hour by himself in balancing probabilities.{1} Can anyone imagine that the tailor and the tanner would be impartial judges? What! the vicious multitude impartial! as if partiality were not ten times more to be feared from men of the same class as the accused than from judges who knew nothing of him personally, lived in another sphere altogether, were irremovable, and conscious of the dignity of their office. But to let a jury decide on crimes against the State and its head, or on misdemeanors of the press, is in a very real sense to set the fox to keep the geese.

{Footnote 1: Boswell's Johnson, 1780, set. 71.}

Everywhere and at all times there has been much discontent with governments, laws, and public regulations; for the most part, however, because men are always ready to make institutions responsible for the misery inseparable from human existence itself; which is, to speak mythically, the curse that was laid on Adam, and through him on the whole race. But never has that delusion been proclaimed in a more mendacious and impudent manner than by the demagogues of the Jetstzeit—of the day we live in. As enemies of Christianity, they are, of course, optimists: to them the world is its own end and object, and accordingly in itself, that is to say, in its own natural constitution, it is arranged on the most excellent principles and forms a regular habitation of bliss. The enormous and glaring evils of the world they attribute wholly to governments: if governments, they think, were to do their duty, there would be a heaven upon earth; in other words, all men could eat, drink, propagate and die, free from trouble, and want. This is what they mean when they talk of the world being "its own end and object"; this is the goal of that "perpetual progress of the human race," and the other fine things which they are never tired of proclaiming.

Formerly it was faith which was the chief support of the throne; nowadays it is credit. The Pope himself is scarcely more concerned to retain the confidence of the faithful than to make his creditors believe in his own good faith. If in times past it was the guilty debt of the world which was lamented, now it is the financial debts of the world which arouse dismay. Formerly it was the Last Day which was prophesied; now it is the {Greek: seisachtheia} the great repudiation, the universal bankruptcy of the nations, which will one day happen; although the prophet, in this as in the other case, entertains a firm hope that he will not live to see it himself.

From an ethical and a rational point of view, the right of possession rests upon an incomparably better foundation than the right of birth; nevertheless, the right of possession is allied with the right of birth and has come to be part and parcel of it, so that it would hardly be possible to abolish the right of birth without endangering the right of possession. The reason of this is that most of what a man possesses he inherited, and therefore holds by a kind of right of birth; just as the old nobility bear the names only of their hereditary estates and by the use of those names do no more than give expression to the fact that they own the estates. Accordingly, all owners of property, if instead of being envious they were wise, ought also to support the maintenance of the rights of birth.

The existence of a nobility has, then, a double advantage: it helps to maintain on the one hand the rights of possession, and on the other the right of birth belonging to the king. For the king is the first nobleman in the country, and, as a general rule, he treats the nobility as his humble relations, and regards them quite otherwise than the commoners, however trusty and well-beloved. It is quite natural, too, that he should have more confidence in those whose ancestors were mostly the first ministers, and always the immediate associates, of his own. A nobleman, therefore, appeals with reason to the name he bears, when on the occurrence of anything to rouse distrust, he repeats his assurance of fidelity and service to the king. A man's character, as my readers are aware, assuredly comes to him from his father. It is a narrow-minded and ridiculous thing not to consider whose son a man is.

FREE-WILL AND FATALISM.

No thoughtful man can have any doubt, after the conclusions reached in my prize-essay on Moral Freedom, that such freedom is to be sought, not anywhere in nature, but outside of it. The only freedom that exists is of a metaphysical character. In the physical world freedom is an impossibility. Accordingly, while our several actions are in no wise free, every man's individual character is to be regarded as a free act. He is such and such a man, because once for all it is his will to be that man. For the will itself, and in itself, and also in so far as it is manifest in an individual, and accordingly constitutes the original and fundamental desires of that individual, is independent of all knowledge, because it is antecedent to such knowledge. All that it receives from knowledge is the series of motives by which it successively develops its nature and makes itself cognizable or visible; but the will itself, as something that lies beyond time, and so long as it exists at all, never changes. Therefore, every man, being what he is and placed in the circumstances which for the moment obtain, but which on their part also arise by strict necessity, can absolutely never do anything else than just what at that moment he does do. Accordingly, the whole course of a man's life, in all its incidents great and small, is as necessarily predetermined as the course of a clock.

The main reason of this is that the kind of metaphysical free act which I have described tends to become a knowing consciousness—a perceptive intuition, which is subject to the forms of space and time. By means of those forms the unity and indivisibility of the act are represented as drawn asunder into a series of states and events, which are subject to the Principle of Sufficient Reason in its four forms—and it is this that is meant by necessity. But the result of it all assumes a moral complexion. It amounts to this, that by what we do we know what we are, and by what we suffer we know what we deserve.

Further, it follows from this that a man's individuality does not rest upon the principle of individuation alone, and therefore is not altogether phenomenal in its nature. On the contrary, it has its roots in the thing-in-itself, in the will which is the essence of each individual. The character of this individual is itself individual. But how deep the roots of individuality extend is one of the questions which I do not undertake to answer.

In this connection it deserves to be mentioned that even Plato, in his own way, represented the individuality of a man as a free act.{1} He represented him as coming into the world with a given tendency, which was the result of the feelings and character already attaching to him in accordance with the doctrine of metempsychosis. The Brahmin philosophers also express the unalterable fixity of innate character in a mystical fashion. They say that Brahma, when a man is produced, engraves his doings and sufferings in written characters on his skull, and that his life must take shape in accordance therewith. They point to the jagged edges in the sutures of the skull-bones as evidence of this writing; and the purport of it, they say, depends on his previous life and actions. The same view appears to underlie the Christian, or rather, the Pauline, dogma of Predestination.

{Footnote 1: Phaedrus and Laws, bk. x.}

But this truth, which is universally confirmed by experience, is attended with another result. All genuine merit, moral as well as intellectual, is not merely physical or empirical in its origin, but metaphysical; that is to say, it is given a priori and not a posteriori; in other words, it lies innate and is not acquired and therefore its source is not a mere phenomenon, but the thing-in-itself. Hence it is that every man achieves only that which is irrevocably established in his nature or is born with him. Intellectual capacity needs, it is true, to be developed just as many natural products need to be cultivated in order that we may enjoy or use them but just as in the case of a natural product no cultivation can take the place of original material, neither can it do so in the case of intellect. That is the reason why qualities which are merely acquired, or learned, or enforced—that is, qualities a posteriori, whether moral or intellectual—are not real or genuine, but superficial only, and possessed of no value. This is a conclusion of true metaphysics, and experience teaches the same lesson to all who can look below the surface. Nay, it is proved by the great importance which we all attach to such innate characteristics as physiognomy and external appearance, in the case of a man who is at all distinguished; and that is why we are so curious to see him. Superficial people, to be sure,—and, for very good reasons, commonplace people too,—will be of the opposite opinion; for if anything fails them; they will thus be enabled to console themselves by thinking that it is still to come.

The world, then, is not merely a battlefield where victory and defeat receive their due recompense in a future state. No! the world is itself the Last Judgment on it. Every man carries with him the reward and the disgrace that he deserves; and this is no other than the doctrine of the Brahmins and Buddhists as it is taught in the theory of metempsychosis.

The question has been raised, What two men would do, who lived a solitary life in the wilds and met each other for the first time. Hobbes, Pufendorf, and Rousseau have given different answers. Pufendorf believed that they would approach each other as friends; Hobbes, on the contrary, as enemies; Rousseau, that they would pass each other by In silence. All three are both right and wrong. This is just a case in which the incalculable difference that there is in innate moral disposition between one individual, and another would make its appearance. The difference is so strong that the question here raised might be regarded as the standard and measure of it. For there are men in whom the sight of another man at once rouses a feeling of enmity, since their inmost nature exclaims at once: That is not me! There are, others in whom the sight awakens immediate sympathy; their inmost nature says: That is me over again! Between the two there are countless degrees. That in this most important matter we are so totally different is a great problem, nay, a mystery.

In regard to this a priori nature of moral character there is matter for varied reflection in a work by Bastholm, a Danish writer, entitled Historical Contributions to the Knowledge of Man in the Savage State. He is struck by the fact that intellectual culture and moral excellence are shown to be entirely independent of each other, inasmuch as one is often found without the other. The reason of this, as we shall find, is simply that moral excellence in no wise springs from reflection, which is developed by intellectual culture, but from the will itself, the constitution of which is innate and not susceptible in itself of any improvement by means of education. Bastholm represents most nations as very vicious and immoral; and on the other hand; he reports that excellent traits of character are found amongst some savage peoples; as, for instance, amongst the Orotchyses, the inhabitants of the island Savu, the Tunguses and the Pelew islanders. He thus attempts to solve the problem, How it is that some tribes are so remarkably good, when their neighbours are all bad, It seems to me that the difficulty may be explained as follows: Moral qualities, as we know, are heritable, and an isolated tribe, such as is described, might take its rise in some one family, and ultimately in a single ancestor who happened to be a good man, and then maintain its purity. Is it not the case, for instance, that on many unpleasant occasions, such as repudiation of public debts, filibustering raids and so on, the English have often reminded the North Americans of their descent from English penal colonists? It is a reproach, however, which can apply only to a small part of the population.

It is marvellous how every man's individuality (that is to say, the union of a definite character with a definite intellect) accurately determines all his actions and thoughts down to the most unimportant details, as though it were a dye which pervaded them; and how, in consequence, one man's whole course of life, in other words, his inner and outer history, turns out so absolutely different from another's. As a botanist knows a plant in its entirety from a single leaf; as Cuvier from a single bone constructed the whole animal, so an accurate knowledge of a man's whole character may be attained from a single characteristic act; that is to say, he himself may to some extent be constructed from it, even though the act in question is of very trifling consequence. Nay, that is the most perfect test of all, for in a matter of importance people are on their guard; in trifles they follow their natural bent without much reflection. That is why Seneca's remark that even the smallest things may be taken as evidence of character, is so true: argumenta morum ex minimis quoque licet capere.{1} If a man shows by his absolutely unscrupulous and selfish behaviour in small things that a sentiment of justice is foreign to his disposition, he should not be trusted with a penny unless on due security. For who will believe that the man who every day shows that he is unjust in all matters other than those which concern property, and whose boundless selfishness everywhere protrudes through the small affairs of ordinary life which are subject to no scrutiny, like a dirty shirt through the holes of a ragged jacket— who, I ask, will believe that such a man will act honourably in matters of meum and tuum without any other incentive but that of justice? The man who has no conscience in small things will be a scoundrel in big things. If we neglect small traits of character, we have only ourselves to blame if we afterwards learn to our disadvantage what this character is in the great affairs of life. On the same principle, we ought to break with so-called friends even in matters of trifling moment, if they show a character that is malicious or bad or vulgar, so that we may avoid the bad turn which only waits for an opportunity of being done us. The same thing applies to servants. Let it always be our maxim: Better alone than amongst traitors.

{Footnote 1: Ep., 52.}

Of a truth the first and foremost step in all knowledge of mankind is the conviction that a man's conduct, taken as a whole, and in all its essential particulars, is not governed by his reason or by any of the resolutions which he may make in virtue of it. No man becomes this or that by wishing to be it, however earnestly. His acts proceed from his innate and unalterable character, and they are more immediately and particularly determined by motives. A man's conduct, therefore, is the necessary product of both character and motive. It may be illustrated by the course of a planet, which is the result of the combined effect of the tangential energy with which it is endowed, and the centripetal energy which operates from the sun. In this simile the former energy represents character, and the latter the influence of motive. It is almost more than a mere simile. The tangential energy which properly speaking is the source of the planet's motion, whilst on the other hand the motion is kept in check by gravitation, is, from a metaphysical point of view, the will manifesting itself in that body.

To grasp this fact is to see that we really never form anything more than a conjecture of what we shall do under circumstances which are still to happen, although we often take our conjecture for a resolve. When, for instance, in pursuance of a proposal, a man with the greatest sincerity, and even eagerness, accepts an engagement to do this or that on the occurrence of a certain future event, it is by no means certain that he will fulfil the engagement; unless he is so constituted that the promise which he gives, in itself and as such, is always and everywhere a motive sufficient for him, by acting upon him, through considerations of honour, like some external compulsion. But above and beyond this, what he will do on the occurrence of that event may be foretold from true and accurate knowledge of his character and the external circumstances under the influence of which he will fall; and it may with complete certainty be foretold from this alone. Nay, it is a very easy prophecy if he has been already seen in a like position; for he will inevitably do the same thing a second time, provided that on the first occasion he had a true and complete knowledge of the facts of the case. For, as I have often remarked, a final cause does not impel a man by being real, but by being known; causa finalis non movet secundum suum esse reale, sed secundum esse cognitum.{1} Whatever he failed to recognize or understand the first time could have no influence upon his will; just as an electric current stop when some isolating body hinders the action of the conductor. This unalterable nature of character, and the consequent necessity of our actions, are made very clear to a man who has not, on any given occasion, behaved as he ought to have done, by showing a lack either of resolution or endurance or courage, or some other quality demanded at the moment. Afterwards he recognizes what it is that he ought to have done; and, sincerely repenting of his incorrect behaviour, he thinks to himself, If the opportunity were offered to me again, I should act differently. It is offered once more; the same occasion recurs; and to his great astonishment he does precisely the same thing over again.{2}

{Footnote 1: Suarez, Disp. Metaph., xxiii.; §§7 and 8.}

{Footnote 2: Cf. World as Will, ii., pp. 251 ff. sqq. (third edition).}

The best examples of the truth in question are in every way furnished by Shakespeare's plays. It is a truth with which he was thoroughly imbued, and his intuitive wisdom expressed it in a concrete shape on every page. I shall here, however, give an instance of it in a case in which he makes it remarkably clear, without exhibiting any design or affectation in the matter; for he was a real artist and never set out from general ideas. His method was obviously to work up to the psychological truth which he grasped directly and intuitively, regardless of the fact that few would notice or understand it, and without the smallest idea that some dull and shallow fellows in Germany would one day proclaim far and wide that he wrote his works to illustrate moral commonplaces. I allude to the character of the Earl of Northumberland, whom we find in three plays in succession, although he does not take a leading part in any one of them; nay, he appears only in a few scenes distributed over fifteen acts. Consequently, if the reader is not very attentive, a character exhibited at such great intervals and its moral identity, may easily escape his notice, even though it has by no means escaped the poet's. He makes the earl appear everywhere with a noble and knightly grace, and talk in language suitable to it; nay, he sometimes puts very beautiful and even elevated passages, into his mouth. At the same time, he is very far from writing after the manner of Schiller, who was fond of painting the devil black, and whose moral approval or disapproval of the characters which he presented could be heard in their own words. With Shakespeare, and also with Goethe, every character, as long as he is on the stage and speaking, seems to be absolutely in the right, even though it were the devil himself. In this respect let the reader compare Duke Alba as he appears in Goethe with the same character in Schiller.

We make the acquaintance of the Earl of Northumberland in the play of Richard II., where he is the first to hatch a plot against the King in favour of Bolingbroke, afterwards Henry IV., to whom he even offers some personal flattery (Act II., Sc. 3). In the following act he suffers a reprimand because, in speaking of the King he talks of him as "Richard," without more ado, but protests that he did it only for brevity's sake. A little later his insidious words induce the King to surrender. In the following act, when the King renounces the crown, Northumberland treats him with such harshness and contempt that the unlucky monarch is quite broken, and losing all patience once more exclaims to him: Fiend, thou torment'st me ere I come to hell! At the close, Northumberland announces to the new King that he has sent the heads of the former King's adherents to London.

In the following tragedy, Henry IV., he hatches a plot against the new King in just the same way. In the fourth act we see the rebels united, making preparations for the decisive battle on the morrow, and only waiting impatiently for Northumberland and his division. At last, there arrives a letter from him, saying that he is ill, and that he cannot entrust his force to anyone else; but that nevertheless the others should go forward with courage and make a brave fight. They do so, but greatly weakened by his absence, they are completely defeated; most of their leaders are captured, and his own son, the valorous Hotspur, falls by the hand of the Prince of Wales.

Again, in the following play, the Second Part of Henry IV., we see him reduced to a state of the fiercest wrath by the death of his son and maddened by the thirst for revenge. Accordingly, he kindles another rebellion, and the heads of it assemble once more. In the fourth act, just as they are about to give battle, and are only waiting for him to join them, there comes a letter saying that he cannot collect a proper force and will therefore seek safety for the present in Scotland; that, nevertheless, he heartily wishes their heroic undertaking the best success. Thereupon they surrender to the King under a treaty which is not kept, and so perish.

So far is character from being the work of reasoned choice and consideration that in any action the intellect has nothing to do but to present motives to the will. Thereafter it looks on as a mere spectator and witness at the course which life takes, in accordance with the influence of motive on the given character. All the incidents of life occur, strictly speaking, with the same necessity as the movement of a clock. On this point let me refer to my prize-essay on The Freedom of the Will. I have there explained the true meaning and origin of the persistent illusion that the will is entirely free in every single action; and I have indicated the cause to which it is due. I will only add here the following teleological explanation of this natural illusion.

Since every single action of a man's life seems to possess the freedom and originality which in truth only belong to his character as he apprehends it and the mere apprehension of it by his intellect is what constitutes his career and since what is original in every single action seems to the empirical consciousness to be always being performed anew, a man thus receives in the course of his career the strongest possible moral lesson. Then, and not before, he becomes thoroughly conscious of all the bad sides of his character. Conscience accompanies every act with the comment: You should act differently, although its true sense is: You could be other than you are. As the result of this immutability of character on the one hand, and, on the other, of the strict necessity which attends all the circumstances in which character is successively placed, every man's course of life is precisely determined from Alpha right through to Omega. But, nevertheless, one man's course of life turns out immeasurably happier, nobler and more worthy than another's, whether it be regarded from a subjective or an objective point of view, and unless we are to exclude all ideas of justice, we are led to the doctrine which is well accepted in Brahmanism and Buddhism, that the subjective conditions in which, as well as the objective conditions under which, every man is born, are the moral consequences of a previous existence.

Macchiavelli, who seems to have taken no interest whatever in philosophical speculations, is drawn by the keen subtlety of his very unique understanding into the following observation, which possesses a really deep meaning. It shows that he had an intuitive knowledge of the entire necessity with which, characters and motives being given, all actions take place. He makes it at the beginning of the prologue to his comedy Clitia. If, he says, the same men were to recur in the world in the way that the same circumstances recur, a hundred years would never elapse without our finding ourselves together once more, and doing the same things as we are doing now—*Se nel mondo tornassino i medesimi uomini, como tornano i medesimi casi, non passarebbono mai cento anni che noi non ci trovassimo un altra volta insieme, a fare le medesime cose che hora.* He seems however to have been drawn into the remark by a reminiscence of what Augustine says in his De Civitate Dei, bk. xii., ch. xiii.

Again, Fate, or the {Greek: eimarmenae} of the ancients, is nothing but the conscious certainty that all that happens is fast bound by a chain of causes, and therefore takes place with a strict necessity; that the future is already ordained with absolute certainty and can undergo as little alteration as the past. In the fatalistic myths of the ancients all that can be regarded as fabulous is the prediction of the future; that is, if we refuse to consider the possibility of magnetic clairvoyance and second sight. Instead of trying to explain away the fundamental truth of Fatalism by superficial twaddle and foolish evasion, a man should attempt to get a clear knowledge and comprehension of it; for it is demonstrably true, and it helps us in a very important way to an understanding of the mysterious riddle of our life. Predestination and Fatalism do not differ in the main. They differ only in this, that with Predestination the given character and external determination of human action proceed from a rational Being, and with Fatalism from an irrational one. But in either case the result is the same that happens which must happen.

On the other hand, the conception of Moral Freedom is inseparable from that of Originality. A man may be said, but he cannot be conceived, to be the work of another, and at the same time be free in respect of his desires and acts. He who called him into existence out of nothing in the same process created and determined his nature—in other words, the whole of his qualities. For no one can create without creating a something, that is to say, a being determined throughout and in all its qualities. But all that a man says and does necessarily proceeds from the qualities so determined; for it is only the qualities themselves set in motion. It is only some external impulse that they require to make their appearance. As a man is, so must he act; and praise or blame attaches, not to his separate acts, but to his nature and being.

That is the reason why Theism and the moral responsibility of man are incompatible; because responsibility always reverts to the creator of man; and it is there that it has its Centre. Vain attempts have been made to make a bridge from one of these incompatibles to the other by means of the conception of moral freedom; but it always breaks down again. What is free must also be original. If our will is free, our will is also the original element, and conversely. Pre-Kantian dogmatism tried to separate these two predicaments. It was thereby compelled to assume two kinds of freedom, one cosmological, of the first cause and the other moral and theological, of human will. These are represented in Kant by the third as well as the fourth antimony of freedom.

On the other hand, in my philosophy the plain recognition of the strictly necessary character of all action is in accordance with the doctrine that what manifests itself even in the organic and irrational world is will. If this were not so, the necessity under which irrational beings obviously act would place their action in conflict with will; if, I mean, there were really such a thing as the freedom of individual action, and this were not as strictly necessitated as every other kind of action. But, as I have just shown, it is this same doctrine of the necessary character of all acts of will which makes it needful to regard a man's existence and being as itself the work of his freedom, and consequently of his will. The will, therefore, must be self-existent; it must possess so-called a-se-ity. Under the opposite supposition all responsibility, as I have shown, would be at an end, and the moral like the physical world would be a mere machine, set in motion for the amusement of its manufacturer placed somewhere outside of it. So it is that truths hang together, and mutually advance and complete one another; whereas error gets jostled at every corner.

What kind of influence it is that moral instruction may exercise on conduct, and what are the limits of that influence, are questions which I have sufficiently examined in the twentieth section of my treatise on the Foundation of Morality. In all essential particulars an analogous influence is exercised by example, which, however, has a more powerful effect than doctrine, and therefore it deserves a brief analysis.

In the main, example works either by restraining a man or by encouraging him. It has the former effect when it determines him to leave undone what he wanted to do. He sees, I mean, that other people do not do it; and from this he judges, in general, that it is not expedient; that it may endanger his person, or his property, or his honour.

He rests content, and gladly finds himself relieved from examining into the matter for himself. Or he may see that another man, who has not refrained, has incurred evil consequences from doing it; this is example of the deterrent kind. The example which encourages a man works in a twofold manner. It either induces him to do what he would be glad to leave undone, if he were not afraid lest the omission might in some way endanger him or injure him in others' opinion; or else it encourages him to do what he is glad to do but has hitherto refrained from doing from fear of danger or shame; this is example of the seductive kind. Finally, example may bring a man to do what he would have otherwise never thought of doing. It is obvious that in this last case example works in the main only on the intellect; its effect on the will is secondary, and if it has any such effect, it is by the interposition of the man's own judgment, or by reliance on the person who presented the example.

The whole influence of example—and it is very strong—rests on the fact that a man has, as a rule, too little judgment of his own, and often too little knowledge, o explore his own way for himself, and that he is glad, therefore, to tread in the footsteps of someone else. Accordingly, the more deficient he is in either of these qualities, the more is he open to the influence of example; and we find, in fact, that most men's guiding star is the example of others; that their whole course of life, in great things and in small, comes in the end to be mere imitation; and that not even in the pettiest matters do they act according to their own judgment. Imitation and custom are the spring of almost all human action. The cause of it is that men fight shy of all and any sort of reflection, and very properly mistrust their own discernment. At the same time this remarkably strong imitative instinct in man is a proof of his kinship with apes.

But the kind of effect which example exercises depends upon a man's character, and thus it is that the same example may possibly seduce one man and deter another. An easy opportunity of observing this is afforded in the case of certain social impertinences which come into vogue and gradually spread. The first time that a man notices anything of the kind, he may say to himself: For shame! how can he do it! how selfish and inconsiderate of him! really, I shall take care never to do anything like that. But twenty others will think: Aha! if he does that, I may do it too.

As regards morality, example, like doctrine, may, it is true, promote civil or legal amelioration, but not that inward amendment which is, strictly speaking, the only kind of moral amelioration. For example, always works as a personal motive alone and assumes, therefore, that a man is susceptible to this sort of motive. But it is just the predominating sensitiveness of a character to this or that sort of motive that determines whether its morality is true and real; though, of whatever kind it is, it is always innate. In general, it may be said that example operates as a means of promoting the good and the bad qualities of a character, but it does not create them and so it is that Seneca's maxim, velle non discitur—will cannot be learned—also holds good here. But the innateness of all truly moral qualities, of the good as of the bad, is a doctrine that consorts better with the metempsychosis of the Brahmins and Buddhists, according to which a man's good and bad deeds follow him from one existence to another like his shadow, than with Judaism. For Judaism requires a man to come into the world as a moral blank, so that, in virtue of an inconceivable free will, directed to objects which are neither to be sought nor avoided—liberum arbitrium indifferentiae—and consequently as the result of reasoned consideration, he may choose whether he is to be an angel or a devil, or anything else that may lie between the two. Though I am well aware what the Jewish scheme is, I pay no attention to it; for my standard is truth. I am no professor of philosophy, and therefore I do not find my vocation in establishing the fundamental ideas of Judaism at any cost, even though they forever bar the way to all and every kind of philosophical knowledge. Liberum arbitrium indifferentiae under the name of moral freedom is a charming doll for professors of philosophy to dandle; and we must leave it to those intelligent, honourable and upright gentlemen.

CHARACTER.

Men who aspire to a happy, a brilliant and a long life, instead of to a virtuous one, are like foolish actors who want to be always having the great parts,—the parts that are marked by splendour and triumph. They fail to see that the important thing is not what or how much, but how they act.

Since a man does not alter, and his moral character remains absolutely the same all through his life; since he must play out the part which he has received, without the least deviation from the character; since neither experience, nor philosophy, nor religion can affect any improvement in him, the question arises, What is the meaning of life at all? To what purpose is it played, this farce in which everything that is essential is irrevocably fixed and determined?

It is played that a man may come to understand himself, that he may see what it is that he seeks and has sought to be; what he wants, and what, therefore, he is. This is a knowledge which must be imparted to him from without. Life is to man, in other words, to will, what chemical re-agents are to the body: it is only by life that a man reveals what he is, and it is only in so far as he reveals himself that he exists at all. Life is the manifestation of character, of the something that we understand by that word; and it is not in life, but outside of it, and outside time, that character undergoes alteration, as a result of the self-knowledge which life gives. Life is only the mirror into which a man gazes not in order that he may get a reflection of himself, but that he may come to understand himself by that reflection; that he may see what it is that the mirror shows. Life is the proof sheet, in which the compositors' errors are brought to light. How they become visible, and whether the type is large or small, are matters of no consequence. Neither in the externals of life nor in the course of history is there any significance; for as it is all one whether an error occurs in the large type or in the small, so it is all one, as regards the essence of the matter, whether an evil disposition is mirrored as a conqueror of the world or a common swindler or ill-natured egoist. In one case he is seen of all men; in the other, perhaps only of himself; but that he should see himself is what signifies.

Therefore, if egoism has a firm hold of a man and master's him, whether it be in the form of joy, or triumph, or lust, or hope, or frantic grief, or annoyance, or anger, or fear, or suspicion, or passion of any kind—he is in the devil's clutches and how he got into them does not matter. What is needful is that he should make haste to get out of them; and here, again, it does not matter how.

I have described character as theoretically an act of will lying beyond time, of which life in time, or character in action, is the development. For matters of practical life, we all possess the one as well as the other; for we are constituted of them both. Character modifies our life more than we think, and it is to a certain extent true that every man is the architect of his own fortune. No doubt it seems as if our lot were assigned to us almost entirely from without, and imparted to us in something of the same way in which a melody outside us reaches the ear. But on looking back over our past, we see at once that our life consists of mere variations on one and the same theme, namely, our character, and that the same fundamental bass sounds through it all. This is an experience which a man can and must make in and by himself.

Not only a man's life, but his intellect too, may be possessed of a clear and definite character, so far as his intellect is applied to matters of theory. It is not every man, however, who has an intellect of this kind; for any such definite individuality as I mean is genius—an original view of the world, which presupposes an absolutely exceptional individuality, which is the essence of genius. A man's intellectual character is the theme on which all his works are variations. In an essay which I wrote in Weimar I called it the knack by which every genius produces his works, however various. This intellectual character determines the physiognomy of men of genius—what I might call the theoretical physiognomy—and gives it that distinguished expression which is chiefly seen in the eyes and the forehead. In the case of ordinary men, the physiognomy presents no more than a weak analogy with the physiognomy of genius. On the other hand, all men possess the practical physiognomy, the stamp of will, of practical character, of moral disposition; and it shows itself chiefly in the mouth.

Since character, so far as we understand its nature, is above and beyond time, it cannot undergo any change under the influence of life. But although it must necessarily remain the same always, it requires time to unfold itself and show the very diverse aspects which it may possess. For character consists of two factors: one, the will-to-live itself, blind impulse, so-called impetuosity; the other, the restraint which the will acquires when it comes to understand the world; and the world, again, is itself will. A man may begin by following the craving of desire, until he comes to see how hollow and unreal a thing is life, how deceitful are its pleasures, what horrible aspects it possesses; and this it is that makes people hermits, penitents, Magdalene's. Nevertheless, it is to be observed that no such change from a life of great indulgence in pleasure to one of resignation is possible, except to the man who of his own accord renounces pleasure. A really bad life cannot be changed into a virtuous one. The most beautiful soul, before it comes to know life from its horrible side, may eagerly drink the sweets of life and remain innocent. But it cannot commit a bad action; it cannot cause others suffering to do a pleasure to itself, for in that case it would see clearly what it would be doing; and whatever be its youth and inexperience it perceives the sufferings of others as clearly as its own pleasures. That is why one bad action is a guarantee that numberless others will be committed as soon as circumstances give occasion for them. Somebody once remarked to me, with entire justice, that every man had something very good and humane in his disposition, and also something very bad and malignant; and that according as he was moved one or the other of them made its appearance. The sight of others' suffering arouses, not only in different men, but in one and the same man, at one moment an inexhaustible sympathy, at another a certain satisfaction; and this satisfaction may increase until it becomes the cruelest delight in pain. I observe in myself that at one moment I regard all mankind with heartfelt pity, at another with the greatest indifference, on occasion with hatred, nay, with a positive enjoyment of their pain.

All this shows very clearly that we are possessed of two different, nay, absolutely contradictory, ways of regarding the world: one according to the principle of individuation, which exhibits all creatures as entire strangers to us, as definitely not ourselves. We can have no feelings for them but those of indifference, envy, hatred, and delight that they suffer. The other way of regarding the world is in accordance with what I may call the Tat-twam-asi— this-is-thyself principle. All creatures are exhibited as identical with us, and so it is pity and love which the sight of them arouses.

The one method separates individuals by impassable barriers; the other removes the barrier and brings the individuals together. The one makes us feel, in regard to every man, that is what I am; the other, that is not what I am. But it is remarkable that while the sight of another's suffering makes us feel our identity with him, and arouses our pity, this is not so with the sight of another's happiness. Then we almost always feel some envy; and even though we may have no such feeling in certain cases,—as, for instance, when our friends are happy,—yet the interest which we take in their happiness is of a weak description and cannot compare with the sympathy which we feel with their suffering. Is this because we recognize all happiness to be a delusion or an impediment to true welfare? No! I am inclined to think that it is because the sight of the pleasure, or the possessions, which are denied to us, arouses envy; that is to say, the wish that we, and not the other, had that pleasure or those possessions.

It is only the first way of looking at the world which is founded on any demonstrable reason. The other is, as it were, the gate out of this world; it has no attestation beyond itself, unless it be the very abstract and difficult proof which my doctrine supplies. Why the first way predominates in one man, and the second in another—though perhaps it does not exclusively predominate in any man; why the one or the other emerges according as the will is moved—these are deep problems. The paths of night and day are close together:

{Greek: Engus gar nuktos de kai aematos eisi keleuthoi.}

It is a fact that there is a great and original difference between one empirical character and another; and it is a difference which, at bottom, rests upon the relation of the individual's will to his intellectual faculty. This relation is finally determined by the degree of will in his father and of intellect in his mother; and the union of father and mother is for the most part an affair of chance. This would all mean a revolting injustice in the nature of the world, if it were not that the difference between parents and son is phenomenal only and all chance is, at bottom, necessity.

As regards the freedom of the will, if it were the case that the will manifested itself in a single act alone, it would be a free act. But the will manifests itself in a course of life, that is to say, in a series of acts. Every one of these acts, therefore, is determined as a part of a complete whole, and cannot happen otherwise than it does happen. On the other hand, the whole series is free; it is simply the manifestation of an individualized will.

If a man feels inclined to commit a bad action and refrains, he is kept back either (1) by fear of punishment or vengeance; or (2) by superstition in other words, fear of punishment in a future life; or (3) by the feeling of sympathy, including general charity; or (4) by the feeling of honour, in other words, the fear of shame; or (5) by the feeling of justice, that is, an objective attachment to fidelity and good-faith, coupled with a resolve to hold them sacred, because they are the foundation of all free intercourse between man and man, and therefore often of advantage to himself as well. This last thought, not indeed as a thought, but as a mere feeling, influences people very frequently. It is this that often compels a man of honour, when some great but unjust advantage has offered him, to reject it with contempt and proudly exclaim I am an honourable man! For otherwise how should a poor man, confronted with the property which chance or even some worse agency has bestowed on the rich, whose very existence it is that makes him poor, feel so much sincere respect for this property, that he refuses to touch it even in his need; and although he has a prospect of escaping punishment, what other thought is it that can be at the bottom of such a man's honesty? He is resolved not to separate himself from the great community of honourable people who have the earth in possession, and whose laws are recognized everywhere. He knows that a single dishonest act will ostracize and proscribe him from that society for ever. No! a man will spend money on any soil that yields him good fruit, and he will make sacrifices for it.

With a good action,—that, every action in which a man's own advantage is ostensibly subordinated to another's,—the motive is either (1) self-interest, kept in the background; or (2) superstition, in other words, self-interest in the form of reward in another life; or (3) sympathy; or (4) the desire to lend a helping hand, in other words, attachment to the maxim that we should assist one another in need, and the wish to maintain this maxim, in view of the presumption that someday we ourselves may find it serve our turn. For what Kant calls a good action done from motives of duty and for the sake of duty, there is, as will be seen, no room at all. Kant himself declares it to be doubtful whether an action was ever determined by pure motives of duty alone. I affirm most certainly that no action was ever so done; it is mere babble; there is nothing in it that could really act as a motive to any man. When he shelters himself behind verbiage of that sort, he is always actuated by one of the four motives which I have described. Among these it is obviously sympathy alone which is quite genuine and sincere.

Good and bad apply to character only à potiori; that is to say, we prefer the good to the bad; but absolutely, there is no such distinction. The difference arises at the point which lies between subordinating one's own advantage to that of another, and not subordinating it. If a man keeps to the exact middle, he is just. But most men go an inch in their regard for others' welfare to twenty yards in regard for their own.

The source of good and of bad character, so far as we have any real knowledge of it, lies in this, that with the bad character the thought of the external world, and especially of the living creatures in it, is accompanied—all the more, the greater the resemblance between them and the individual self—by a constant feeling of not I, not I, not I.

Contrarily, with the good character (both being assumed to exist in a high degree) the same thought has for its accompaniment, like a fundamental bass, a constant feeling of I, I, I. From this spring benevolence and a disposition to help all men, and at the same time a cheerful, confident, and tranquil frame of mind, the opposite of that which accompanies the bad character.

The difference, however, is only phenomenal, although it is a difference which is radical. But now we come to the hardest of all problems: How is it that, while the will, as the thing-in-itself, is identical, and from a metaphysical point of view one and the same in all its manifestations, there is nevertheless such an enormous difference between one character and another?—the malicious, diabolical wickedness of the one, and set off against it, the goodness of the other, showing all the more conspicuously. How is it that we get a Tiberius, a Caligula, a Carcalla, a Domitian, a Nero; and on the other hand, the Antonine's, Titus, Hadrian, Nerva? How is it that among the animals, nay, in a higher species, in individual animals, there is a like difference?—the malignity of the cat most strongly developed in the tiger; the spite of the monkey; on the other hand, goodness, fidelity and love in the dog and the elephant. It is obvious that the principle of wickedness in the brute is the same as in man.

We may to some extent modify the difficulty of the problem by observing that the whole difference is in the end only one of degree. In every living creature, the fundamental propensities and instincts all exist, but they exist in very different degrees and proportions. This, however, is not enough to explain the facts.

We must fall back upon the intellect and its relation to the will; it is the only explanation that remains. A man's intellect, however, by no means stands in any direct and obvious relation with the goodness of his character. We may, it is true, discriminate between two kinds of intellect: between understanding, as the apprehension of relation in accordance with the Principle of Sufficient Reason, and cognition, a faculty akin to genius, which acts more directly, is independent of this law, and passes beyond the Principle of Individuation. The latter is the faculty which apprehends Ideas, and it is the faculty which has to do with morality. But even this explanation leaves much to be desired. Fine minds are seldom fine souls was the correct observation of Jean Paul, although they are never the contrary. Lord Bacon, who, to be sure, was less a fine soul than a fine mind, was a scoundrel.

I have declared space and time to be part of the Principle of Individuation, as it is only space and time that make the multiplicity of similar objects a possibility. But multiplicity itself also admits of variety; multiplicity and diversity are not only quantitative, but also qualitative. How is it that there is such a thing as qualitative diversity, especially in ethical matters? Or have I fallen into an error the opposite of that in which Leibnitz fell with his identitas indiscernibilium?

The chief cause of intellectual diversity is to be found in the brain and nervous system. This is a fact which somewhat lessens the obscurity of the subject. With the brutes the intellect and the brain are strictly adapted to their aims and needs. With man alone there is now and then, by way of exception, a superfluity, which, if it is abundant, may yield genius. But ethical diversity, it seems, proceeds immediately from the will. Otherwise, ethical character would not be above and beyond time, as it is only in the individual that intellect and will are united. The will is above and beyond time, and eternal; and character is innate; that is to say, it is sprung from the same eternity, and therefore it does not admit of any but a transcendental explanation.

Perhaps someone will come after me who will throw light into this dark abyss.

MORAL INSTINCT.

An act done by instinct differs from every other kind of act in that an understanding of its object does not precede it but follows upon it. Instinct is therefore a rule of action given à priori. We may be unaware of the object to which it is directed, as no understanding of it is necessary to its attainment. On the other hand, if an act is done by an exercise of reason or intelligence, it proceeds according to a rule which the understanding has itself devised for the purpose of carrying out a preconceived aim. Hence it is that action according to rule may miss its aim, while instinct is infallible.

On the à priori character of instinct we may compare what Plato says in the Philebus. With Plato instinct is a reminiscence of something which a man has never actually experienced in his lifetime; in the same way as, in the Phaedo and elsewhere, everything that a man learns is regarded as a reminiscence. He has no other word to express the à priori element in all experience.

There are, then, three things that are à priori:

(1) Theoretical Reason, in other words, the conditions which make all experience possible.

(2) Instinct, or the rule by which an object promoting the life of the senses may, though unknown, be attained.

(3) The Moral Law, or the rule by which an action takes place without any object.

Accordingly rational or intelligent action proceeds by a rule laid down in accordance with the object as it is understood. Instinctive action proceeds by a rule without an understanding of the object of it. Moral action proceeds by a rule without any object at all.

Theoretical Reason is the aggregate of rules in accordance with which all my knowledge—that is to say, the whole world of experience—necessarily proceeds. In the same manner Instinct is the aggregate of rules in accordance with which all my action necessarily proceeds if it meets with no obstruction. Hence it seems to me that Instinct may most appropriately be called practical reason, for like theoretical reason it determines the must of all experience.

The so-called moral law, on the other hand is only one aspect of the better consciousness, the aspect which it presents from the point of view of instinct. This better consciousness is something lying beyond all experience, that is, beyond all reason, whether of the theoretical or the practical kind, and has nothing to do with it; whilst it is in virtue of the mysterious union of it and reason in the same individual that the better consciousness comes into conflict with reason, leaving the individual to choose between the two.

In any conflict between the better consciousness and reason, if the individual decides for reason, should it be theoretical reason, he becomes a narrow, pedantic philistine; should it be practical, a rascal.

If he decides for the better consciousness, we can make no further positive affirmation about him, for if we were to do so, we should find ourselves in the realm of reason; and as it is only what takes place within this realm that we can speak of at all it follows that we cannot speak of the better consciousness except in negative terms.

This shows us how it is that reason is hindered and obstructed; that theoretical reason is suppressed in favour of genius and practical reason in favour of virtue. Now the better consciousness is neither theoretical nor practical; for these are distinctions that only apply to reason. But if the individual is in the act of choosing, the better consciousness appears to him in the aspect which it assumes in vanquishing and overcoming the practical reason (or instinct, to use the common word). It appears to him as an imperative command, an ought. It so appears to him, I say; in other words, that is the shape which it takes for the theoretical reason which renders all things into objects and ideas. But in so far as the better consciousness desires to vanquish and overcome the theoretical reason, it takes no shape at all; on the simple ground that, as it comes into play, the theoretical reason is suppressed and becomes the mere servant of the better consciousness. That is why genius can never give any account of its own works.

In the morality of action, the legal principle that both sides are to be heard must not be allowed to apply; in other words, the claims of self and the senses must not be urged. Nay, on the contrary, as soon as the pure will has found expression, the case is closed; nec audienda altera pars.

The lower animals are not endowed with moral freedom. Probably this is not because they show no trace of the better consciousness which in us is manifested as morality, or nothing analogous to it; for, if that were so, the lower animals, which are in so many respects like ourselves in outward appearance that we regard man as a species of animal, would possess some raison d'être entirely different from our own, and actually be, in their essential and inmost nature, something quite other than ourselves. This is a contention which is obviously refuted by the thoroughly malignant and inherently vicious character of certain animals, such as the crocodile, the hyaena, the scorpion, the snake, and the gentle, affectionate, and contented character of others, such as the dog. Here, as in the case of men, the character, as it is manifested, must rest upon something that is above and beyond time. For, as Jacob Böhme says,{1} there is a power in every animal which is indestructible, and the spirit of the world draws it into itself, against the final separation at the Last Judgment. Therefore, we cannot call the lower animals free and the reason why we cannot do so is that they are wanting in a faculty which is profoundly subordinate to the better consciousness in its highest phase, I mean reason. Reason is the faculty of supreme comprehension, the idea of totality. How reason manifests itself in the theoretical sphere Kant has shown, and it does the same in the practical: it makes us capable of observing and surveying the whole of our life, thought, and action, in continual connection and therefore of acting according to general maxims, whether those maxims originate in the understanding as prudential rules, or in the better consciousness as moral laws.

{Footnote 1: Epistles, 56.}

If any desire or passion is aroused in us, we, and in the same way the lower animals, are for the moment filled with this desire; we are all anger, all lust, all fear; and in such moments neither the better consciousness can speak, nor the understanding consider the consequences. But in our case reason allows us even at that moment to see our actions and our life as an unbroken chain,—a chain which connects our earlier resolutions, or, it may be, the future consequences of our action, with the moment of passion which now fills our whole consciousness. It shows us the identity of our person, even when that person is exposed to influences of the most varied kind, and thereby we are enabled to act according to maxims. The lower animal is wanting in this faculty; the passion which seizes it completely dominates it and can be checked only by another passion—anger, for instance, or lust, by fear; even though the vision that terrifies does not appeal to the senses but is present in the animal only as a dim memory and imagination.

Men, therefore, may be called irrational, if, like the lower animals, they allow themselves to be determined by the moment.

So far, however, is reason from being the source of morality that it is reason alone which makes us capable of being rascals, which the lower animals cannot be. It is reason which enables us to form an evil resolution and to keep it when the provocation to evil is removed; it enables us, for example, to nurse vengeance. Although at the moment that we have an opportunity of fulfilling our resolution the better consciousness may manifest itself as love or charity, it is by force of reason, in pursuance of some evil maxim, that we act against it. Thus, Goethe says that a man may use his reason only for the purpose of being more bestial than any beast:

> *Er hat Vernunft, doch braucht er sie allein*
> *Um theirischer als jedes Thier zu sein.*

For not only do we, like the beasts, satisfy the desires of the moment, but we refine upon them and stimulate them in order to prepare the desire for the satisfaction.

Whenever we think that we perceive a trace of reason in the lower animals, it fills us with surprise. Now our surprise is not excited by the good and affectionate disposition which some of them exhibit—we recognize that as something other than reason— but by some action in them which seems to be determined not by the impression of the moment, but by a resolution previously made and kept. Elephants, for instance, are reported to have taken premeditated revenge for insults long after they were suffered; lions, to have requited benefits on an opportunity tardily offered. The truth of such stories has, however, no bearing at all on the question, What do we mean by reason? But they enable us to decide whether in the lower animals there is any trace of anything that we can call reason.

Kant not only declares that all our moral sentiments originate in reason, but he lays down that reason, in my sense of the word, is a condition of moral action; as he holds that for an action to be virtuous and meritorious it must be done in accordance with maxims, and not spring from a resolve taken under some momentary impression. But in both contentions, he is wrong. If I resolve to take vengeance on someone and when an opportunity offers, the better consciousness in the form of love and humanity speaks its word, and I am influenced by it rather than by my evil resolution, this is a virtuous act, for it is a manifestation of the better consciousness. It is possible to conceive of a very virtuous man in whom the better consciousness is so continuously active that it is never silent, and never allows his passions to get a complete hold of him. By such consciousness he is subject to a direct control, instead of being guided indirectly, through the medium of reason, by means of maxims and moral principles. That is why a man may have weak reasoning powers and a weak understanding and yet have a high sense of morality and be eminently good; for the most important element in a man depends as little on intellectual as it does on physical strength. Jesus says, Blessed are the poor in spirit. And Jacob Böhme has the excellent and noble observation: Whoso lies quietly in his own will, like a child in the womb, and lets himself be led and guided by that inner principle from which he is sprung, is the noblest and richest on earth.{1}

{Footnote 1: Epistles, 37.}

ETHICAL REFLECTIONS.

The philosophers of the ancient world united in a single conception a great many things that had no connection with one another. Of this every dialogue of Plato's furnishes abundant examples. The greatest and worst confusion of this kind is that between ethics and politics. The State and the Kingdom of God, or the Moral Law, are so entirely different in their character that the former is a parody of the latter, a bitter mockery at the absence of it. Compared with the Moral Law the State is a crutch instead of a limb, an automaton instead of a man.

The principle of honour stands in close connection with human freedom. It is, as it were, an abuse of that freedom. Instead of using his freedom to fulfil the moral law, a man employs his power of voluntarily undergoing any feeling of pain, of overcoming any momentary impression, in order that he may assert his self-will, whatever be the object to which he directs it. As he thereby shows that, unlike the lower animals, he has thoughts which go beyond the welfare of his body and whatever makes for that welfare, it has come about that the principle of honour is often confused with virtue. They are regarded as if they were twins. But wrongly; for although the principle of honour is something which distinguishes man from the lower animals, it is not, in itself, anything that raises him above them. Taken as an end and aim, it is as dark a delusion as any other aim that springs from self. Used as a means, or casually, it may be productive of good; but even that is good which is vain and frivolous. It is the misuse of freedom, the employment of it as a weapon for overcoming the world of feeling, that makes man so infinitely more terrible than the lower animals; for they do only what momentary instinct bids them; while man acts by ideas, and his ideas may entail universal ruin before they are satisfied.

There is another circumstance which helps to promote the notion that honour, and virtue are connected. A man who can do what he wants to do shows that he can also do it if what he wants to do is a virtuous act. But that those of our actions which we are ourselves obliged to regard with contempt are also regarded with contempt by other people serves more than anything that I have here mentioned to establish the connection. Thus, it often happens that a man who is not afraid of the one kind of contempt is unwilling to undergo the other. But when we are called upon to choose between our own approval and the world's censure, as may occur in complicated and mistaken circumstances, what becomes of the principle of honour then?

Two characteristic examples of the principle of honour are to be found in Shakespeare's Henry VI., Part II., Act IV., Sc. 1. A pirate is anxious to murder his captive instead of accepting, like others, a ransom for him; because in taking his captive he lost an eye, and his own honour and that of his forefathers would in his opinion be stained if he were to allow his revenge to be bought off as though he were a mere trader. The prisoner, on the other hand, who is the Duke of Suffolk, prefers to have his head grace a pole than to uncover it to such a low fellow as a pirate, by approaching him to ask for mercy.

Just as civic honour—in other words, the opinion that we deserve to be trusted—is the palladium of those whose endeavour it is to make their way in the world on the path of honourable business, so knightly honour—in other words, the opinion that we are men to be feared—is the palladium of those who aim at going through life on the path of violence; and so it was that knightly honour arose among the robber-knights and other knights of the Middle Ages.

A theoretical philosopher is one who can supply in the shape of ideas for the reason, a copy of the presentations of experience; just as what the painter sees he can reproduce on canvas; the sculptor, in marble; the poet, in pictures for the imagination, though they are pictures which he supplies only in sowing the ideas from which they sprang.

A so-called practical philosopher, on the other hand, is one who, contrarily, deduces his action from ideas. The theoretical philosopher transforms life into ideas. The practical philosopher transforms ideas into life; he acts, therefore, in a thoroughly reasonable manner; he is consistent, regular, deliberate; he is never hasty or passionate; he never allows himself to be influenced by the impression of the moment.

And indeed, when we find ourselves among those full presentations of experience, or real objects, to which the body belongs—since the body is only an objectified will, the shape which the will assumes in the material world—it is difficult to let our bodies be guided, not by those presentations, but by a mere image of them, by cold, colourless ideas, which are related to experience as the shadow of Orcus to life; and yet this is the only way in which we can avoid doing things of which we may have to repent.

The theoretical philosopher enriches the domain of reason by adding to it; the practical philosopher draws upon it, and makes it serve him.

According to Kant the truth of experience is only a hypothetical truth. If the suppositions which underlie all the intimations of experience—subject, object, time, space, and causality—were removed, none of those intimations would contain a word of truth. In other words, experience is only a phenomenon; it is not knowledge of the thing-in-itself.

If we find something in our own conduct at which we are secretly pleased, although we cannot reconcile it with experience, seeing that if we were to follow the guidance of experience, we should have to do precisely the opposite, we must not allow this to put us out otherwise we should be ascribing an authority to experience which it does not deserve, for all that it teaches rests upon a mere supposition. This is the general tendency of the Kantian Ethics.

Innocence is in its very nature stupid. It is stupid because the aim of life (I use the expression only figuratively, and I could just as well speak of the essence of life, or of the world) is to gain a knowledge of our own bad will, so that our will may become an object for us, and that we may undergo an inward conversion. Our body is itself our will be objectified; it is one of the first and foremost of objects, and the deeds that we accomplish for the sake of the body show us the evil inherent in our will. In the state of innocence, where there is no evil because there is no experience, man is, as it were, only an apparatus for living, and the object for which the apparatus exists is not yet disclosed. An empty form of life like this, a stage untenanted, is in itself, like the so-called real world, null and void; and as it can attain a meaning only by action, by error, by knowledge, by the convulsions of the will, it wears a character of insipid stupidity. A golden age of innocence, a fools' paradise, is a notion that is stupid and unmeaning, and for that very reason in no way worthy of any respect. The first criminal and murderer, Cain, who acquired a knowledge of guilt, and through guilt acquired a knowledge of virtue by repentance, and so came to understand the meaning of life, is a tragical figure more significant, and almost more respectable, than all the innocent fools in the world put together.

If I had to write about modesty I should say: I know the esteemed public for which I have the honour to write far too well to dare to give utterance to my opinion about this virtue. Personally, I am quite content to be modest and to apply myself to this virtue with the utmost possible circumspection. But one thing I shall never admit—that I have ever required modesty of any man, and any statement to that effect I repel as a slander.

The paltry character of most men compels the few who have any merit or genius to behave as though they did not know their own value, and consequently did not know other people's want of value; for it is only on this condition that the mob acquiesces in tolerating merit. A virtue has been made out of this necessity, and it is called modesty. It is a piece of hypocrisy, to be excused only because other people are so paltry that they must be treated with indulgence.

Human misery may affect us in two ways, and we may be in one of two opposite moods in regard to it.

In one of them, this misery is immediately present to us. We feel it in our own person, in our own will which, imbued with violent desires, is everywhere broken, and this is the process which constitutes suffering. The result is that the will increases in violence, as is shown in all cases of passion and emotion; and this increasing violence comes to a stop only when the will turns and gives way to complete resignation, in other words, is redeemed. The man who is entirely dominated by this mood will regard any prosperity which he may see in others with envy, and any suffering with no sympathy.

In the opposite mood human misery is present to us only as a fact of knowledge, that is to say, indirectly. We are mainly engaged in looking at the sufferings of others, and our attention is withdrawn from our own. It is in their person that we become aware of human misery; we are filled with sympathy; and the result of this mood is general benevolence, philanthropy. All envy vanishes, and instead of feeling it, we are rejoiced when we see one of our tormented fellow-creatures experience any pleasure or relief.

After the same fashion we may be in one of two opposite moods in regard to human baseness and depravity. In the one we perceive this baseness indirectly, in others. Out of this mood arise indignation, hatred, and contempt of mankind. In the other we perceive it directly, in ourselves. Out of it there arises humiliation, nay, contrition.

In order to judge the moral value of a man, it is very important to observe which of these four moods predominate in him. They go in pairs, one out of each division. In very excellent characters the second mood of each division will predominate.

The categorical imperative, or absolute command, is a contradiction. Every command is conditional. What is unconditional and necessary is a must, such as is presented by the laws of nature.

It is quite true that the moral law is entirely conditional. There is a world and a view of life in which it has neither validity nor significance. That world is, properly speaking, the real world in which, as individuals, we live; for every regard paid to morality is a denial of that world and of our individual life in it. It is a view of the world, however, which does not go beyond the principle of sufficient reason and the opposite view proceeds by the intuition of Ideas.

If a man is under the influence of two opposite but very strong motives, A and B, and I am greatly concerned that he should choose A, but still more that he should never be untrue to his choice, and by changing his mind betray me, or the like, it will not do for me to say anything that might hinder the motive B from having its full effect upon him, and only emphasize A; for then I should never be able to reckon on his decision. What I have to do is, rather, to put both motives before him at the same time, in as vivid and clear a way as possible, so that they may work upon him with their whole force. The choice that he then makes is the decision of his inmost nature and stands firm to all eternity. In saying I will do this; he has said I must do this. I have got at his will, and I can rely upon its working as steadily as one of the forces of nature. It is as certain as fire kindles and water wets that he will act according to the motive which has proved to be stronger for him. Insight and knowledge may be attained and lost again; they may be changed, or improved, or destroyed; but will cannot be changed. That is why I apprehend, I perceive, I see, is subject to alteration and uncertainty; I will, pronounced on a right apprehension of motive, is as firm as nature itself. The difficulty, however, lies in getting at a right apprehension. A man's apprehension of motive may change or be corrected or perverted; and on the other hand, his circumstances may undergo an alteration.

A man should exercise an almost boundless toleration and placability, because if he is capricious enough to refuse to forgive a single individual for the meanness or evil that lies at his door, it is doing the rest of the world a quite unmerited honour.

But at the same time the man who is every one's friend is no one's friend. It is quite obvious what sort of friendship it is which we hold out to the human race and to which it is open to almost every man to return, no matter what he may have done.

With the ancient's friendship was one of the chief elements in morality. But friendship is only limitation and partiality; it is the restriction to one individual of what is the due of all mankind, namely, the recognition that a man's own nature and that of mankind are identical. At most it is a compromise between this recognition and selfishness.

A lie always has its origin in the desire to extend the dominion of one's own will over other individuals, and to deny their will in order the better to affirm one's own. Consequently, a lie is in its very nature the product of injustice, malevolence, and villainy. That is why truth, sincerity, candour, and rectitude are at once recognized and valued as praiseworthy and noble qualities; because we presume that the man who exhibits them entertains no sentiments of injustice or malice, and therefore stands in no need of concealing such sentiments. He who is open cherishes nothing that is bad.

There is a certain kind of courage which springs from the same source as good-nature. What I mean is that the good-natured man is almost as clearly conscious that he exists in other individuals as in himself. I have often shown how this feeling gives rise to good-nature. It also gives rise to courage, for the simple reason that the man who possesses this feeling cares less for his own individual existence, as he lives almost as much in the general existence of all creatures. Accordingly, he is little concerned for his own life and its belongings. This is by no means the sole source of courage for it is a phenomenon due to various causes. But it is the noblest kind of courage, as is shown by the fact that in its origin it is associated with great gentleness and patience. Men of this kind are usually irresistible to women.

All general rules and precepts fail, because they proceed from the false assumption that men are constituted wholly, or almost wholly, alike; an assumption which the philosophy of Helvetius expressly makes. Whereas the truth is that the original difference between individuals in intellect and morality is immeasurable.

The question as to whether morality is something real is the question whether a well-grounded counter-principle to egoism actually exists.

As egoism restricts concern for welfare to a single individual, viz., the man's own self, the counter-principle would have to extend it to all other individuals.

It is only because the will is above and beyond time that the stings of conscience are ineradicable, and do not, like other pains, gradually wear away. No! an evil deed weighs on the conscience years afterwards as heavily as if it had been freshly committed.

Character is innate, and conduct is merely its manifestation; the occasion for great misdeeds comes seldom; strong counter-motives keep us back; our disposition is revealed to ourselves by our desires, thoughts, emotions, when it remains unknown to others. Reflecting on all this, we might suppose it possible for a man to possess, in some sort, an innate evil conscience, without ever having done anything very bad.

Don't do to others what you wouldn't like done to yourself. This is, perhaps, one of those arguments that prove, or rather ask, too much. For a prisoner might address it to a judge.

Stupid people are generally malicious, for the very same reason as the ugly and the deformed.

Similarly, genius and sanctity are akin. However simple-minded a saint may be, he will nevertheless have a dash of genius in him and however many errors of temperament, or of actual character, a genius may possess, he will still exhibit a certain nobility of disposition by which he shows his kinship with the saint.

The great difference between Law without and Law within, between the State and the Kingdom of God, is very clear. It is the State's business to see that everyone should have justice done to him; it regards men as passive beings, and therefore takes no account of anything but their actions. The Moral Law, on the other hand, is concerned that everyone should do justice; it regards men as active and looks to the will rather than the deed. To prove that this is the true distinction let the reader consider what would happen if he were to say, conversely, that it is the State's business that everyone should do justice, and the business of the Moral Law that everyone should have justice done to him. The absurdity is obvious.

As an example of the distinction, let me take the case of a debtor and a creditor disputing about a debt which the former denies. A lawyer and a moralist are present and show a lively interest in the matter. Both desire that the dispute should end in the same way, although what they want is by no means the same. The lawyer says, I want this man to get back what belongs to him; and the moralist, I want that man to do his duty.

It is with the will alone that morality is concerned. Whether external force hinders or fails to hinder the will from working does not in the least matter. For morality the external world is real only in so far as it is able or unable to lead and influence the will. As soon as the will is determined, that is, as soon as a resolve is taken, the external world and its events are of no further moment and practical do not exist. For if the events of the world had any such reality—that is to say, if they possessed a significance in themselves, or any other than that derived from the will which is affected by them—what a grievance it would be that all these events lie in the realm of chance and error! It is, however, just this which proves that the important thing is not what happens, but what is willed. Accordingly, let the incidents of life be left to the play of chance and error, to demonstrate to man that he is as chaff before the wind.

The State concerns itself only with the incidents—with what happens; nothing else has any reality for it. I may dwell upon thoughts of murder and poison as much as I please: the State does not forbid me, so long as the axe and rope control my will and prevent it from becoming action.

Ethics asks: What are the duties towards others which justice imposes upon us? in other words, What must I render? The Law of Nature asks: What need I not submit to from others? that is, What must I suffer? The question is put, not that I may do no injustice, but that I may not do more than every man must do if he is to safeguard his existence and, than every man will approve being done, in order that he may be treated in the same way himself; and, further, that I may not do more than society will permit me to do. The same answer will serve for both questions, just as the same straight line can be drawn from either of two opposite directions, namely, by opposing forces; or, again, as the angle can give the sine, or the sine the angle.

It has been said that the historian is an inverted prophet. In the same way it may be said that a teacher of law is an inverted moralist (viz., a teacher of the duties of justice), or that politics are inverted ethics, if we exclude the thought that ethics also teaches the duty of benevolence, magnanimity, love, and so on. The State is the Gordian knot that is cut instead of being untied; it is Columbus' egg which is made to stand by being broken instead of balanced, as though the business in question were to make it stand rather than to balance it. In this respect the State is like the man who thinks that he can produce fine weather by making the barometer go up.

The pseudo-philosophers of our age tell us that it is the object of the State to promote the moral aims of mankind. This is not true; it is rather the contrary which is true. The aim for which mankind exists—the expression is parabolic—is not that a man should act in such and such a manner; for all opera operata, things that have actually been done, are in themselves matters of indifference. No! the aim is that the Will, of which every man is a complete specimen—nay, is the very Will itself—should turn whither it needs to turn; that the man himself (the union of Thought and Will) should perceive what this will is, and what horrors it contains; that he should show the reflection of himself in his own deeds, in the abomination of them. The State, which is wholly concerned with the general welfare, checks the manifestation of the bad will, but in no wise checks the will itself; the attempt would be impossible. It is because the State checks the manifestation of his will that a man very seldom sees the whole abomination of his nature in the mirror of his deeds. Or does the reader actually suppose there are no people in the world as bad as Robespierre, Napoleon, or other murderers? Does he fail to see that there are many who would act like them if only they could?

Many a criminal die more quietly on the scaffold than many a non-criminal in the arms of his family. The one has perceived what his will is and has discarded it. The other has not been able to discard it, because he has never been able to perceive what it is. The aim of the State is to produce a fool's paradise, and this is in direct conflict with the true aim of life, namely, to attain a knowledge of what the will, in its horrible nature, really is.

Napoleon was not really worse than many, not to say most, men. He was possessed of the very ordinary egoism that seeks its welfare at the expense of others. What distinguished him was merely the greater power he had of satisfying his will, and greater intelligence, reason, and courage; added to which, chance gave him a favourable scope for his operations. By means of all this he did for his egoism what a thousand other men would like to do for theirs but cannot. Every feeble lad who by little acts of villainy gains a small advantage for himself by putting others to some disadvantage, although it may be equally small, is just as bad as Napoleon.

Those who fancy that retribution comes after death would demand that Napoleon should by unutterable torments pay the penalty for all the numberless calamities that he caused. But he is no more culpable than all those who possess the same will, unaccompanied by the same power.

The circumstance that in his case this extraordinary power was added allowed him to reveal the whole wickedness of the human will; and the sufferings of his age, as the necessary obverse of the medal, reveal the misery which is inextricably bound up with this bad will. It is the general manipulation of this will that constitutes the world. But it is precisely that it should be understood how inextricably the will to live is bound up with, and is really one and the same as, this unspeakable misery, that is the world's aim and purpose; and it is an aim and purpose which the appearance of Napoleon did much to assist. Not to be an unmeaning fools' paradise but a tragedy, in which the will to live understands itself and yields—that is the object for which the world exists. Napoleon is only an enormous mirror of the will to live.

The difference between the man who causes suffering and the man who suffers it, is only phenomenal. It is all a will to live, identical with great suffering; and it is only by understanding this that the will can mend and end.

What chiefly distinguishes ancient from modern times is that in ancient times, to use Napoleon's expression, it was affairs that reigned: les paroles aux choses. In modern times this is not so. What I mean is that in ancient times the character of public life, of the State, and of Religion, as well as of private life, was a strenuous affirmation of the will to live. In modern times it is a denial of this will, for such is the character of Christianity. But now while on the one hand that denial has suffered some abatement even in public opinion, because it is too repugnant to human character, on the other what is publicly denied is secretly affirmed. Hence it is that we see half measures and falsehood everywhere; and that is why modern times look so small beside antiquity.

The structure of human society is like a pendulum swinging between two impulses, two evils in polar opposition, despotism, and anarchy. The further it gets from the one, the nearer it approaches the other. From this the reader might hit on the thought that if it were exactly midway between the two, it would be right. Far from it. For these two evils are by no means equally bad and dangerous. The former is incomparably less to be feared; its ills exist in the main only as possibilities, and if they come at all it is only one among millions that they touch. But, with anarchy, possibility and actuality are inseparable; its blows fall on every man every day. Therefore, every constitution should be a nearer approach to a despotism than to anarchy; nay, it must contain a small possibility of despotism.

LIST OF TITLES WITH ISBN NO.

ISBN	TITLE
9788194914129	1984
9789390575220	1984 & Animal Farm (2In1)
9789390575572	1984 & Animal Farm (2In1): The International Best-Selling Classics
9789390575848	35 Sonnets
9789390575329	A Clergyman's Daughter
9789390575923	A Study In Scarlet
9789390896097	A Tale Of Two Cities
9789390896837	Abide in Christ
9789390896202	Abraham Lincoln
9789390896912	Absolute Surrender
9789390896608	African American Classic Collection
9789390575305	Aldous Huxley: The Collected Works
9789390896141	An Autobiography of M. K. Gandhi
9789390575886	Animal Farm
9789390575619	Animal Farm & The Great Gatsby (2In1)
9789390575626	Animal Farm & We
9789390896158	Anna Karenina
9789390575534	Antic Hay
9789390896165	Antony & Cleopatra
9789390896172	As I Lay Dying
9789390896226	As You like it
9789390575671	At Your Command
9789390575350	Awakened Imagination
9789390575114	Be What You Wish
9789390896233	Believe In yourself
9789390896998	Best of Charles Darwin: The Origin of Species & Autobiography
9789390896684	Best Of Horror : Dracula And Frankenstein
9789390575503	Best Of Mark Twain (The Adventures of Tom Sawyer AND The Adventures of Huckleberry Finn)
9789390896769	Black History Collection
9789390575756	Brave New World, Animal Farm & 1984 (3in1)

9789390896240	Brother Karamzov
9789390575053	Bulleh Shah Poetry
9789390575725	Burmese Days
9789390896257	Bushido
9789390896066	Can't Hurt Me
9788194914112	Chanakya Neeti: With The Complete Sutras
9789390896042	Crime and Punishment
9789390575527	Crome Yellow
9789390575046	Down and Out in Paris and London
9789390896844	Dracula
9789390575442	Emersons Essays: The Complete First & Second Series (Self-Reliance & Other Essays)
9789390575749	Emma
9789390575817	Essential Tozer Collection - The Pursuit of God & The Purpose of Man
9789390896578	Fascism What It Is and How to Fight It
9789390575688	Feeling is the Secret
9789390575190	Five Lessons
9789390575954	Frankenstein
9789390575237	Franz Kafka: Collected Works
9789390575282	Franz Kafka: Short Stories
9789390575060	George Orwell Collected Works
9789390575077	George Orwell Essays
9789390575213	George Orwell Poems
9788194914150	Greatest Poetry Ever Written Vol 1
9788194914143	Greatest Poetry Ever Written Vol 1
9789390896301	Gulliver's Travel
9789390575961	Gunaho Ka Devta
9789390575893	H. P. Lovecraft Selected Stories Vol 1
9789390575978	H. P. Lovecraft Selected Stories Vol 2
9789390896059	Hamlet
9789390575022	His Last Bow: Some Reminiscences of Sherlock Holmes
9789390896134	History of Western Philosophy
9789390575121	Homage To Catalonia

9789390896219	How to develop self-confidence and Improve public Speaking
9789390896295	How to enjoy your life and your Job
9789390575633	How to own your own mind
9789390896318	How to read Human Nature
9789390896325	How to sell your way through the life
9789390896370	How to use the laws of mind
9789390896387	How to use the power of prayer
9789390896028	How to win friends & Influence People
9788194824176	How To Win Friends and Influence People
9789390896103	Humility The Beauty of Holiness
9789390896653	Imperialism the Highest Stage of Capitalism
9789390575084	In Our Time
9789390575169	In Our Time & Three Stories and Ten poems
9789390575145	James Allen: The Collected Works
9789390896189	Jesus Himself
9789390575480	Jo's Boys
9789390896394	Julius Caesar
9789390575404	Keep the Aspidistra Flying
9789390896400	Kidnapped
9789390896424	King Lear
9789390575824	Lady Susan
9789390896455	Law of Success
9789390896264	Lincoln The Unknown
9789390575565	Little Men
9789390575640	Little Women
9788194914174	Lost Horizon
9789390896462	Macbeth
9789390896929	Man Eaters of Kumaon
9789390896523	Man The Dwelling Place of God
9789390896349	Man The Dwelling Place of God
9789390575909	Mansfield Park
9788194914136	Manto Ki 25 Sarvshreshth Kahaniya
9789390896509	Marxism, Anarchism, Communism
9789390575664	Mathematical Principles of Natural Philosophy

9788194914198	Meditations
9789390575800	Mein Kampf
9789390575794	Memory How To Develop, Train, And Use It
9789390896486	Mind Power
9789390896585	Money
9789390575039	Mortal Coils
9789390575770	My Life and Work
9789390896035	Narrative of the Life of Frederick Douglass
9789390575152	Neville Goddard: The Collected Works
9789390575985	Northanger Abbey
9789390896530	Notes From Underground
9789390896547	Oliver Twist
9789390575459	On War
9789390575541	One, None and a Hundred Thousand
9789390896554	Othelo
9789390575435	Out Of This World
9789390575015	Persuasion
9789390575510	Prayer The Art Of Believing
9789390575091	Pride and Prejudice
9789390896561	Psychic Perception
9789390575381	Rabindranath Tagore - 5 Best Short Stories Vol 2
9789390575367	Rabindranath Tagore - Short Stories (Masters Collections Including The Childs Return)
9789390575374	Rabindranath Tagore 5 Best Short Stories Vol 1 (Including The Childs Return
9789390896622	Romeo & Juliet
9789390896127	Sanatana Dharma
9789390575596	Seedtime & Harvest
9789390896639	Selected Stories of Guy De Maupassant
9789390575206	Self-Reliance & Other Essays
9789390575176	Sense and Sensibility
9789390575299	Shyamchi Aai
9789390896738	Socialism Utopian and Scientific
9789390896646	Success Through a Positive Mental Attitude
9789390575428	The Adventures of Huckleberry Finn

9789390575183	The Adventures of Sherlock Holmes
9789390575343	The Adventures of Tom Sawyer
9789390896691	The Alchemy Of Happiness
9789390575862	The Art Of Public Speaking
9789390896288	The Autobiography Of Charles Darwin
9788194914181	The Best of Franz Kafka: The Metamorphosis & The Trial
9789390575008	The Call Of Cthulhu and Other Weird Tales
9789390575107	The Case-Book of Sherlock Holmes
9789390896110	The Castle Of Otranto
9789390896745	The Communist Manifesto
9789390575589	The Complete Fiction of H. P. Lovecraft
9789390575497	The Complete Works of Florence Scovel Shinn
9789390896820	The Conquest of Breard
9789390896813	The Diary of a Young Girl
9789390896332	The Diary of a Young Girl The Definitive Edition of the Worlds Most Famous Diary
9789390575701	The Great Gatsby, Animal Farm & 1984 (3In1)
9789390575312	The Greatest Works Of George Orwell (5 Books) Including 1984 & Non-Fiction
9789390575992	The Hound of Baskervilles
9789390896707	The Idiot
9789390896714	The Invisible Man
9789390575657	The Knowledge of the holy
9789390575558	The Law & the Promise
9789390896721	The Law Of Attraction
9789390896776	The Leader in you
9789390896363	The Life of Christ
9789390896196	The Man-Eating Leopard of Rudraprayag
9789390896783	The Master Key to Riches
9789390575268	The Memoirs Of Sherlock Holmes
9789390896479	The Midsummer Night's Dream
9789390575466	The Mill On The Floss
9789390896790	The Miracles of your mind
9789390896660	The Mutual Aid A Factor in Evolution
9789390896448	The Origin of Species

9789390896905	The Peter Kropotkin Anthology The Conquest of Bread & Mutual Aid A Factor of Evolution
9789390896806	The Picture of Dorian Gray
9789390896271	The Picture of Dorian Gray
9789390575275	The Power Of Awareness
9789390896356	The Power of Concentration
9788194824169	The Power of Positive Thinking
9789390575411	The Power of the Spoken Word
9788194914105	The Power Of Your Subconscious Mind
9789390896899	The Power of Your Subconscious Mind
9789390896417	The Principles of Communism
9789390575787	The Psychology Of Mans Possible Evolution
9789390896615	The Psychology of Salesmanship
9789390575732	The Pursuit of God
9789390575398	The Pursuit of Happiness
9789390896851	The Quick and Easy Way to effective Speaking
9789390575947	The Return Of Sherlock Holmes
9789390575138	The Road To Wigan Pier
9789390896981	The Root of the Righteous
9789390575855	The Science Of Being Well
9788194914167	The Science Of Getting Rich, The Science Of Being Great & The Science Of Being Well (3In1)
9789390896011	The Screwtape Letters
9789390896073	The Screwtape Letters
9789390575336	The Secret Door to Success
9789390575695	The Secret Of Imagining
9789390896868	The Secret Of Success
9789390896431	The Seven Last Words
9789390575930	The Sign of the Four
9789390896004	The Sonnets
9789390896516	The Souls of Black Folk
9789390896875	The Sound and The Fury
9789390575244	The State and Revolution
9789390896882	The Story of My Life
9789390896936	The Story Of Oriental Philosophy

9789390896752	The Strange Case of Dr. Jekyll and Mr. Hyde
9789390896943	The Tempest
9789390575916	The Valley Of Fear
9789390575879	The Wind in the willows
9789390896080	The Wind in the willows
9789390575763	Their eyes were watching gofd
9789390575831	Three Stories
9789390896950	Twelfth Night
9789390896592	Twelve Years a Slave
9789390896677	Up from Slavery
9789390896974	Value Price and Profit
9789390896967	Wake Up and Live
9789390896493	With Christ in the School of Prayer
9789390575602	Your Faith is Your Fortune
9789390575473	Your Infinite Power To Be Rich
9789390575251	Your Word is Your Wand
9789390575718	Youth
9789391316099	A Christmas Carol
9789391316105	A Doll's House
9789391316501	A Passage to India
9789391316709	A Portrait of the Artist as a Young Man
9789391316112	A Tale of Two Cities
9789391316747	A Tear and a Smile
9789391316167	Agnes Gray
9789391316174	Alice's Adventures in Wonderland
9789391316136	Anandamath
9789391316181	Anne Of Green Gables
9789391316754	Anthem
9789391316198	Around The World in 80 Days
9789391316013	As A Man Thinketh
9789391316242	Autobiography of a Yogi
9789391316266	Beyond Good and Evil
9789391316761	Bleak House
9789391316778	Chitra, a Play in One Act
9789391316310	David Copperfield

9789391316075	Demian
9789391316785	Dubliners
9789391316051	Favourite Tales from the Arabian Nights
9789391316235	Gitanjali
9789391316068	Gravity
9789391316150	Great Speeches of Abraham Lincoln
9789391316662	Guerilla Warfare
9789391316839	Kim
9789391316822	Mother
9789391316211	My Childhood
9789391316846	Nationalism
9789391316327	Oliver Twist
9789391316853	Pygmalion
9789391316334	Relativity: The Special and the General Theory
9789391316389	Scientific Healing Affirmation
9789391316341	Sons and Lovers
9789391316587	Tales from India
9789391316372	Tess of The D'Urbervilles
9789391316396	The Awakening and Selected Stories
9789391316402	The Bhagvad Gita
9789391316303	The Book of Enoch
9789391316228	The Canterville Ghost
9789391316907	The Dynamic Laws of Prosperity
9789391316006	The Great Gatsby
9789391316860	The Hungry Stones and Other Stories
9789391316433	The Idiot
9789391316440	The Importance of Being Earnest
9789391316297	The Light of Asia
9789391316914	The Madman His Parables and Poems
9789391316457	The Odyssey
9789391316921	The Picture of Dorian Gray
9789391316464	The Prince
9789391316938	The Prophet
9789391316945	The Republic
9789391316518	The Scarlet Letter

9789391316143	The Seven Laws of Teaching
9789391316525	The Story of My Experiments with Truth
9789391316532	The Tales of the Mother Goose
9789391316549	The Thirty Nine Steps
9789391316594	The Time Machine
9789391316600	The Turn of the Screw
9789391316983	The Upanishads
9789391316617	The Yellow Wallpaper
9789391316426	The Yoga Sutras of Patanjali
9789391316990	Ulysses
9789391316624	Utopia
9789391316679	Vanity Fair
9789391316020	What Is To Be Done
9789391316686	Within A Budding Grove
9789391316693	Women in Love

9 789362 056481